W9-CHS-835

SPORTS
IN
AMERICA

SPORTS
IN
AMERICA
Fascination and Blemishes

Glenn W. Ferguson

SANTA FE

Illustrations by Bob Eggers

Sunstone books may be purchased for educational, business, or sales promotional use. For information please write: Special Markets Department, Sunstone Press, P.O. Box 2321, Santa Fe, New Mexico 87504-2321.

Library of Congress Cataloging-in-Publication Data:

Ferguson, Glenn W.
   Sports in America: fascination and blemishes / Glenn W. Ferguson.
     p. cm.
   ISBN: 0-86534-419-1 (hardcover)
   1. Sports—United States—History. 2. Sports—Social aspects—United States.
   3. Athletes— United States—History. I. Title.
   GV583.F47 2004
   796'.0973—dc22

                  2004005786

Published in

WWW.SUNSTONEPRESS.COM
SUNSTONE PRESS / POST OFFICE BOX 2321 / SANTA FE, NM 87504-2321 / USA
(505) 988-4418 / *ORDERS ONLY* (800) 243-5644 / FAX (505) 988-1025

To our children,
Bruce, Sherry, and Scott,
stars in the Fergolympics.

CONTENTS

PROLOGUE

This book represents a committed effort of more than thirty years to capture the essence of sports. In 1970, I started keeping a daily journal which became a series of short essays rather than a diary. One of the subjects was my personal participation in sports. The Journal excerpts have provided a subjective flavor to review the evolution and impact of a variety of sports.

Sports have always been an integral part of my life. Through injuries, and the choice of a career, the detours were fundamental and limiting. My personal participation was not the controlling factor; however, without that exposure, I would have been less able to focus on the impact of athletics.

Through the environment of sports, I have had the privilege of working with, and becoming friends with, a bevy of people who have represented a comparable sports commitment. In looking at the stars who have emerged in contemporary sports, it is obvious that the values have changed, and are continuing to change, appreciably.

Without sports, my life would have included a critical void. If I were to begin now, my disappointments would have been profound. The essential reforms in sports must begin.

I

The Author as a Participant

I have the greatest respect for a person who excels in any athletic endeavor. Success may be related partially to genes, parental interest, mentors, the quality of coaching and competition, and good fortune. To be adjudged superior in any sport deserves special recognition.

During my formative years, I participated in several sports. I had natural ability in a few, coupled with a competitive nature and a generous dose of diligence. Although I have many fond memories of athletics, I never experienced the elation of being "number one." Injuries and inferior coaching contributed to that reality.

In 1941, at age 12, I played right field in one game, as a substitute, in a summer baseball league, high school level game, in Central Square, New York, near my home in Syracuse. The team was composed predominately of high school athletes from the region. Because I was able to throw a hardball accurately for distance, I was allowed to join the team and to play a few innings with "the big boys." Although I served as a pinch runner before assuming my position in the outfield, I was too inexperienced to be entrusted with a bat.

For two years, I played catch with my father who was a second baseman in a Lynchburg, Virginia, industrial league. As my speed increased, my father acquired a catcher's mitt. I dug a small hole in the driveway which served as a pitcher's mound, and he would call balls and strikes in a fictional game. As part of the orientation, he taught me how to throw a curve and a knuckleball.

By the summer of 1943, I could pitch with a semblance of precision. In the summer league, my team, Nottingham, defeated Bellevue Heights 18 to 4. Defense was not the hallmark of either team's effort, but I did pitch the complete game, struck out nine, and the four runs scored on errors.

During the summer, I also worked as a caretaker for the Drumlins Country Club tennis courts, and as a golf caddy, and enjoyed the fringe benefits with an occasional match in both sports. In Syracuse, there were not any "Little Leagues" in any sport, and formal games in basketball and baseball were not played until ninth grade. In basketball, I played guard for Charles Andrews Junior High School and was second highest scorer.

Between the ages of 12 and 14, I played right wing for the teenage ice hockey team at Drumlins rink. Games were arranged against other teams in the area. Prior to high school, my family moved to the Washington, D.C., area, and I never played another game of hockey.

At Bethesda-Chevy Chase High School in suburban Maryland, I participated in football, basketball, track and baseball, and won varsity letters in each sport. In football, I was quarterback in a single-wing formation (tailback), and I completed 70 percent of the passes which I threw in my senior year. In the last game, I ran back the kickoff 95 yards for the winning score. Of greater importance, the fingers of my passing hand were damaged, and I never regained my earlier facility.

In basketball, I was a starting guard. Because of my speed, I was the roving center in a zone defense and was able to intercept a significant number of passes. I led the team in steals and assists. My scoring ability was limited, but our team qualified for the Metropolitan Washington quarter-finals.

In track, although there was not any formal team and my training was limited, I qualified for the 100-yard dash finals, but did not win, in the District of Columbia outdoor high school championships.

In baseball, I was a "southpaw" and played center field when I was not pitching. I was the leading hitter with a .304 average (not a heavy hitter). In my final effort, I pitched a no-hit game against Georgetown Prep. Bethesda won 2-0, and my double scored both runs. I struck out 11 batters, but to demonstrate my lack of consistency, I walked six.

In the summer before college, I played golf on the weekends. In a short vacation, I spent several days with a friend in Buffalo, Minnesota. We played in a Minnesota State Golf Tournament, and I won the consolation bracket in my flight. My drives were lengthy, and for many years, I held the distance record at the White Flint Club in Rockville, Maryland.

As a freshman at Cornell University in Ithaca, New York, I played football and baseball. As a wingback in another single wing formation, I passed frequently and did more running than in high school. Again, I suffered debilitating injuries to my left (passing) hand and twisted my ankle severely. I was advised to ignore my football dreams.

In baseball, I pitched on the freshman team. The *Cornell Daily Sun* accused me of having a "great assortment of stuff." In the summer of 1947, following my freshman year, I had a tryout with the Washington Senators before a game in Griffith Stadium in Washington, D.C. Ossie Bluege, one of the most outstanding major league shortstops, was the manager. He provided me with a Senators uniform and introduced me to the outstanding catcher, Wes Ferrell, who caught my offerings while Manager Bluege watched. The tryout occurred just before the scheduled game, and I pitched on the warm-up mound in front of the dugout. My father was in the stands. I was not a picture of self-confidence. Initially, my curve would not break. Mr. Ferrell calmed me down, and the breaking pitches came alive. It was suggested that I might be assigned to Orlando, the Washington farm team in the Florida International League. It was grand to watch the major league game that followed and to experience Walter Mitty dreams.

In the spring of 1948, while pitching for the Cornell Varsity in the glass-domed cage in the late March pre-season, the coach shouted for me to throw as hard as I could. March in Ithaca approximates Alaska, even in a glassed infield. I was reluctant, but I assumed that he knew his trade. I developed a calcified elbow. The elbow did not respond to treatment, and my fastball disappeared.

In the final game of the season, with my parents in attendance, I pitched for the last time. By then, I was barely able to roll the ball up to the plate. On my final pitch, the batter hit a home run over the right field fence, and I was through pitching. In the period following World War II, "warming up" adequately was not considered essential for a pitcher. Of greater importance, the "coach" was not qualified to deal with pitchers.

Without football or baseball potential, for three years I concentrated on the track team. I was able to make the varsity in the 100 and 220 yard dashes. I usually ran the 100 yard dash in the winter and spring dual meets, in the Heptagonals, and in the Penn Relays. Most of the competition was Ivy League, but I did run the 100 against the University of Michigan at Ann Arbor. I never won a dash event, but I scored points for Cornell, ran in the 440 yard relay, and was awarded a varsity letter.

Before and after a stint in Korea as an Air Force Psychological Warfare Officer, I played golf, baseball, and tennis at Clark Air Force Base in the Philippines. In baseball, although I was unable to pitch, I played left field. In the last game, in my last time at bat, I hit a home run to left field. It was my only home run as a player, but I considered it a partial retribution for my last outing as a Cornell pitcher.

In golf, I played regularly on sand greens and shot in the mid to high 70s. In tennis, in 1953, after returning from Korea, I qualified for the Philippine National tournament in Baguio. After advancing a few rounds, I lost to a rated player who returned every shot with a high lob. When he utilized that tactic, I was unable to retain my "cool."

During the past half century, I attempted to play golf and tennis for several years. There was never time to maintain a level of skill. In Chicago, it took a minimum of three hours to complete eighteen holes in golf. I quit summarily never completing another round. With the exception of occasional tennis, and infrequent paddle racquets, I have concentrated on running (really jogging) four to six miles three times per week. In the last few years in Santa Fe, a series of "old age" infirmities have intervened. I now concentrate on walking, light exercises, and reverie.

Obviously, this personal sports history has been prepared in order to establish minimal credentials and to set the stage for substantive comments concerning the world of sports. In a limited sports career, I flirted with several options and did not excel in any. Except for golf, I enjoyed them all. In that sport, with limited time, I was "playing myself" rather than an opponent or a team. Following a double bogey, my day was ruined. In other sports, my mistakes could be absorbed in context.

To excel in athletics is a tribute to the individual; however, injuries can become a reality. The sport pages are filled with tales of physical limitations.

Of greater importance, the meaning and role of sports in American society have changed appreciably in the last fifty years. Joy for the participant and the spectator are in jeopardy. Moral fiber is now secondary to jingoism and commercialism. The innocence of my early sports experience has disappeared.

2

Major Sports

Baseball—The National Pastime

Five minutes watching cricket will establish the parentage of baseball. In the early nineteenth century, using discarded cricket balls, and occasionally even cricket bats, baseball was played in the United States in variable forms. From 1840-1880, cricket, in its purest version, was played by scores of teams on the Eastern Seaboard. A bit of cricket was borrowed in formulating the rules of American baseball.

Conventional wisdom has placed in granite the origin of American baseball. The sport was created by Abner Doubleday. In 1839, the first game was played at Cooperstown, New York, the situs of the Baseball Hall of Fame.

Semi-reliable evidence suggests that the first game was played on June 4, 1838, at Beachville, Ontario. Although a game was undoubtedly played a year prior to the first game at Cooperstown, earlier in the nineteenth century, baseball was played at several locations in the northeast. Prior to 1838, there were innumerable games in New Jersey, and it is reasonably certain that Doubleday was exposed to the game in that state.

The American penchant for being first, independent of the facts, applies to our national pastime. It would be edifying to discover from whom Henry Ford borrowed his idea. The French had operational automobiles many years before the Model "T" was on display.

The intricacies of baseball have evolved slowly. The changes have been profound. The baseball bat has become a precision instrument. The ball has become more lively which partially explains the home run craze. For more than a century, the rules have reflected more precision every year. Television introduced a commitment to the complexity of the game, and Jackie Robinson represented a new race in the major leagues. When I was a youngster, there were eight teams in each of two major leagues. It was relatively easy to recognize the players and to follow the statistical evolution. After expansion, there are now thirty teams; it is impossible to keep up with the names of the players; skill is in short supply, and a pitcher who wins twenty games is a celebrity.

There is only one statistic that does not bear scrutiny. Now that the Colorado team plays in Denver at 5,000 feet, home runs leave the stadium in great profusion. Altitude reflects a natural variable like wind in Chicago or rain in Seattle.

The one incongruity that the baseball authorities could easily standardize is the distance to the fences in the outfield. When there were eight teams in each league, the distances to the fences ranged as follows: right field—258 to 366 feet; center field—375 to 505 feet; left field—279 to 405 feet. With the approximate doubling of the total number of teams, the variation in the distance to the fences has not been improved.

It would be interesting to review a statistical analysis of the number of home runs hit with the present distances to the fences as a stabilizing factor. Baseball is remarkably complex, and the statistics are fascinating. If the distance to the fences were uniform, the home run craze would be related immediately to a meaningful standard.

Major league baseball has nurtured an amazing array of colorful names. Although each sport has a patch of exotic names, baseball is unique. For illustrative purposes, the following are cited: Van Lingle Mungo, Duke

Snider, Babe Ruth, Peewee Reese, Arky Vaughan, Tris Speaker, Frank Frisch, Dizzy and Daffy Dean, Cy Young, Nellie Fox, Sparky Anderson, Sal Maglie, Casey Stengel, Ty Cobb, Honus Wagner, Hoyt Wilhelm, Grover Cleveland Alexander, Nap Lajoie, Branch Rickey, Nolan Ryan, Satchel Paige, Willie Keeler, Sandy Koufax, Lloyd Waner, Carl Hubbell, Willie Mays, Tinker to Evers to Chance (a double play combination), Tug McGraw, Yogi Berra, Moose Skowron and Goose Goslin. The list is endless. The nicknames are truly unique because most of the surnames are short and exotic.

With regard to baseball evolution, Satchel Paige put it aptly: "Never look back; something may be gaining on you." (At the probable age of fifty, Satchel was the first Black pitcher in the major leagues.)

While running, I fantasize. For each lap, I secure another victory on the mound for one of my heroes or myself (in my make believe major league career). If I complete the requisite five-mile run, I have achieved thirty victories and an asterisk in the pages of baseball memorabilia. To increase the drama, I begin the run with thirty losses already recorded. For each milestone completed, usually a partial lap, a loss is deleted while a win is secured.

Whenever I am reluctant to share my idiosyncracies, I recognize that I have company. Fox television once featured a movie about a 12-year-old Little League scrub baseball player, of limited ability, who suffered a serious accident while attempting to catch a ball in the outfield. The fall damaged his throwing arm. When it healed, it became a veritable pitching machine. The Chicago Cubs scouts discovered that he could throw a baseball with greater velocity than established limits. He was signed to a contract, and he proceeded to overpower opposing batters. Eventually, another accident restored his pre-teenage throwing limitations.

Recently, I followed Route 80 to Van Meter, Iowa, twelve miles west of Des Moines. Bob Feller, the Hall of Fame pitcher for the Cleveland Indians, was born and raised in Van Meter. When I was a boy, Feller was one of my few heroes. As a left-handed pitcher, the hero-worship was not misplaced.

Leaving Van Meter High School at age seventeen, Feller became an immediate starting pitcher for the Cleveland Indians. His success was astounding and included three no-hit games. During three years of service in World War II, he was decorated as a naval gunner. In spite of the extensive interruption of his pitching career, after the war he returned to the Indians, continued his distinguished performance, and was elected to the Baseball Hall of Fame.

At the Bob Feller Museum, former Big League players make periodic summer visits to conduct baseball clinics. The museum is small but includes important memorabilia concerning a distinguished local citizen.

Statistics, Strategy, and Demeanor

Baseball may be the only sport where those who read about the games, listen to them on the radio, or watch them on television are as avid as the fans who attend the live performances. The precise, complex, unlimited statistics have established this unique manifestation of support.

Baseball statistics are endlessly fascinating. Lou Gehrig's record of 2,130 games played in succession was considered inviolate. In 1995, when he voluntarily remained out of a game, Cal Ripkin had played 2,632 consecutive major league games. The differential involves approximately three years of playing in every game.

Joe Dimaggio married Marilyn Monroe. In spite of that fact, he is remembered more fondly for hitting safely in 56 consecutive games. That record is unlikely to be broken. In 1998, in a single week, Mark McGwire hit his 60th home run equaling Babe Ruth's season record, the 61st matching Roger Maris, and the 62nd establishing a new major league record. For two generations, Babe Ruth's record was considered beyond reach. When McGwire hit his 70th homer, it was alleged that the record was not subject to change. With Sammy Sosa in the wings, the competition solidified baseball as the national pastime and even assisted President Bill Clinton in the polls. Wait another minute! In 2001, Barry Bonds exceeded

McGwire's record by three home runs, and the sky (and steroids) are now the limit.

To further illustrate the preoccupation with baseball statistics, Joe Dimaggio was never thrown out while running from first to third base. It is tempting to ask whether he took the requisite number of chances.

There is always a novel statistical approach introduced in baseball. In 1977, based on his lifetime interest in baseball statistics, Bill James of Lawrence, Kansas, inaugurated a newsletter which in 1980 was converted to "Baseball Abstract." The "Abstract" became a unique resource for baseball devotees and team leaders who were interested in precise statistical observations.

After serving as a part-time consultant to major league baseball teams, in 2002, James accepted a full-time commitment with the Boston Red Sox. Basically, he prepared statistical analyses of the performance of relief pitchers. To date, his findings have represented only limited value; however, it is probable that the Red Sox management will find the statistical conclusions useful in employing relevant strategy. Sporting the title of "Baseball Operations Advisor," James reflects the modern hype of contemporary major sports.

The national pastime is not confined to numbers. In other sports, it would be unusual for players or coaches to replicate the immortal wisdom of baseball: Yogi Berra ("A sense of deja vu all over again"), Casey Stengel ("The game ain't over til it's over"), or Dizzy Dean after pitching a 1-0 shutout ("The game was closer than the score indicated").

Baseball has warts, but they have been absorbed by meaningful old age rather than the knee-jerk ravings associated with less venerable sports. Baseball statistics are cranial, useful, and fun.

At the risk of alienating a nation of positive thinkers, the statistical preoccupation of sportswriters and fans should be extended to the compilation of meaningful negative statistics. Occasionally, the names of the worst hitters of the month are buried in a chart at the bottom of the last sports page, but that statistic only whets the appetite.

In baseball, comparable lists should be compiled for the most strikeouts by batters, the most batters hit by pitchers, the most failures to steal a base, and the most ejections for pitchers who throw at the heads of batters.

I recognize that the weekly statistics, compiled by a few solid newspapers, incorporate each player in major league baseball including those with the fewest hits, most pitching losses, and greatest number of errors. These negative statistics should be emphasized in the same manner that home runs, runs batted in, stolen bases, earned run averages, and arguments with umpires are prominently displayed.

If a chart were to incorporate the players who were sent to the minors, a critical new statistical variable would be available for incessant discussions at social gatherings.

At the same time, the love affair of baseball writers with player injuries should be offset by a monthly list of the few baseball players who did not complain about physical problems.

Returning to my principal theme, a listing of the managers who were ejected during the previous month would insure essential perspective. Negativism regarding baseball statistics might generate positive reactions from many baseball devotees.

Before leaving the baseball preoccupation with statistics, I would like to suggest an All-Star approach incorporating the antithesis of statistics. Professional athletes should be selected for All-Star teams that feature demeanor including courtesy and the absence of hubris. Obviously, our choice would be limited by the prejudice of the media. Courtesy, and a subdued reaction to stress, seldom tempt a sportswriter, or can be easily converted to statistics; therefore, the choices would be limited. Acceptable temperament used to be a virtue.

○ ○ ○

A few football "grunts" may dispute the statement, but strategy in baseball is unique in sports. Most sports fans are enamored with the personal interest stories; the ambience of the stadium; baiting referees, players and fans, and the score. In baseball, there are devotees of comparable persuasion, but fans generally enjoy the remarkable substance, complexity, and subtlety of the sport.

Baseball, the most esoteric sport, incorporates intellectually stimulating strategy. It can be interpreted superficially by an observant fan; however, few fans are able to experience the depth of feeling and understanding associated with a balk; a hit and run play; a double steal; the infield fly rule with men on base; the importance of a "change up" pitch including the knuckleball and the forkball; the decision to walk a batter; critical choices in removing a pitcher; the ostensibly easy decision to pinch hit, or the importance of the myriad signals which are conveyed from the dugout or from the third base coaching box. The impact of a home run, and the difference of opinion with an umpire, can be appreciated by the typical fan. The intellectual joy of intricate baseball strategy is understood by few aficionados.

Unless beer and hot dogs are a preoccupation while attending a game, most baseball fans understand significant components of strategy. On the other hand, sports eggheads and selected writers (e.g., George Will) are attracted by the constantly emerging nuances. Few sports have generated the number of books dealing with strategy; a poem with the intensity of "Casey at the Bat," or the loyalty and understanding of the fans who supported the Dodgers or the early New York Yankees.

Baseball is my favorite sport. A lifetime of interest and observation is still insufficient to fully comprehend the distinctions which characterize the game. When "play ball" is shouted, or the crack of the ball against the bat echoes in the stadium, an unusual experience is at hand.

Following dinner in the Great Moments Room at Yankee Stadium (in the photographic presence of Ruth, Gehrig, Dimaggio, Mantle, Maris, et al.), we witnessed a game with the Baltimore Orioles from management's private box. I dislike biting the hand that feeds me (free tickets), but several of the Yankee players, managers, and owners of the last thirty years are my non-favorites in baseball.

In every sport, style and humility are, or should be, a *sine qua non* for excellence. Generally, the New York Yankees, except for the presence of one contemporary manager, have been devoid of these ingredients.

When the New York Yankees lose a game, I am delighted. My bride maintains that such a sentiment is perverted, and that I should always be "for" something rather than "against." That standard is comparable to the adage which my mother made famous: "If you cannot say something nice, don't say anything at all." If that edict were followed, the human voice would never have been developed as an instrument.

It is my thesis that overt opposition is a true reaction. There is nothing nefarious about elation which is related to the failure of a cause, group, or team which you consider evil, egotistical, gross, or unfeeling. For years, the New York Yankees have reflected many of those traits. Since the departure of Casey Stengel, who was competent and funny, the New York Mets run a close second.

During the past generation, the individual and collective behavior of the New York Yankees, and particularly their owner, has been the antithesis of what professional sports should represent. When they lose, comparative goodness has been vindicated, and I feel more positive about the world. Since somebody has to lose, I am confident that the Yankees are the outstanding candidate.

Two of my least favorite sports figures in the professional baseball world supported each other. George Steinbrunner, owner of the New York Yankees, and pitcher David Wells, who returned to the Yankees from Toronto, were mutual admirers.

Wells is a cult hero. "Boomer" appealed to many of the fans in the bleachers. He is rotund (with a shape like Babe Ruth) and engages in questionable extracurricular activities. Wells, who may have stayed up until dawn on game days, engaged in a recent physical caper in an Upper East Side diner. At a minimum, a butcher's knife was involved. In a previous early morning diner altercation, he lost two teeth.

Before assessing punishment for the most recent offense, the Yankee General Manager actually called other major league teams to establish the fact that they do not enforce home game curfews. Based on this fundamental research, Wells was not subjected to punishment. If his season record were four wins and nineteen losses, a penalty might have been levied.

Wells is consistent. During his initial Yankee spring training stint, he arrived at the field with a broken hand received in another bar tussle. He also missed the second game of a recent double header because of a dentist's appointment. Following the dawn diner incident, when his name was announced at Yankee Stadium, he received a sustained, rousing cheer from the bleachers.

Obviously, our hero is cherished because he is winning and because his lifestyle appeals to a certain element in the typical crowd. When an athlete, usually a professional, excels and behaves in a less than professional manner, he or she can be adored by the masses. In professional basketball, Dennis Rodman and Charles Barkley were perennial selections. If Wells, as a Yankee, had exercised a modicum of restraint, and restricted his beverage consumption, he might have been selected as an All Star; however, he would have been ignored by the bleacher crowd.

In the early years of my marriage, before children and job responsibilities became primary commitments, I watched a variety of college and professional sports on television.

During the 2001 World Series, because I was retired (except for the joys of writing) and recovering from surgery, I opted to watch the New York Yankees and the Arizona Diamondbacks. I anticipated devoting only a few hours to the pursuit. Three of my favorite players were engaged: Roger Clemens of the Yankees and Messrs. Shilling and Grace of the Diamondbacks. The quality of the performance by both teams captured my attention for the entire series.

Following the September 11, 2001, terrorist attacks at the World Trade Center, and as my deep concern for those affected in New York City subsided, I found that my identification with many components of the city increased. For example, a temporary attachment to the New York Yankees, and their low-key manager, was created.

The World Series was captivating. The home team won each of the first six games. Only two games were decided by more than a single run. Clemens won the third game and was leading late in the seventh game when he was removed. Johnson and Shilling were designated the most valuable players. For the Diamondbacks, Mark Grace, a superb, aging player, whom I followed when he was a Chicago Cub, was a picture of his surname at first base.

In the seventh game, with the hint of Yankee victory, in the ninth inning, Arizona scored two runs against Rivera, the premium reliever for the Yankees.

It was immaterial which team won. The series was exhilarating, and both managers employed the ultimate in strategy. In spite of the commercials, I was grateful. Watching the World Series is a unique experience.

In the arcane world of baseball strategy, why does not the manager of the visiting team in the National league utilize a pinch hitter, who has an aptitude for getting on base, as the lead-off hitter in the top of the first inning? The regular lead-off batter would be on deck. The pitcher would then replace the lead-off pinch hitter in the lineup and begin the normal pitching assignment in the bottom of the first inning.

This tactic would reduce a pitcher's appearances at the plate. He would bat in the "tenth" position rather than ninth in the order. The loss of a light-hitting pinch hitter, who has a proclivity for getting on base, would not be a significant factor. If he were a utility infielder, on a rare occasion, his absence later in the game might be relevant. Normally, pinch hitters represent power. In this situation, a utility infielder who lacks power, but who possesses speed and walks occasionally, might be an ideal candidate.

This ploy could only be utilized for away games. At home, the pitcher would be used in the top of the first inning, and the pinch hitter would have to replace the pitcher in order to bat.

With more than eighty games scheduled away during a major league season, the pitchers would be batting approximately eighty fewer times. A margin of a run could make a critical difference. The absence of a utility infielder might be relatively unimportant.

Commercialism in Action

The Detroit Tigers professional baseball team is enjoying a new stadium. Comerica Inc. paid $66 million for the honor of associating its name with the stadium. To help defray the initial cost, the corporation sold red paving bricks which will be entombed in the entry plaza.

For $99, a fan of the Tigers (there are a few still living in Detroit) purchases a single brick engraved in gold letters with the name of the donor and any selected special message. For $250, a fan purchases a larger brick which will be displayed in the same area. To complete the offer, a fan with limited financial means takes the replica of a brick home for $50. If the Tigers hit a losing streak, that category of brick will probably be thrown from the bleachers. If the Tigers win a few games, the cheap bricks will probably be sold to the highest bidder. In the meantime, Comerica Inc. was nominated for the 2001 crass commercialism award.

In Sydney, Australia, they commemorate authors and artists with special plaques embedded in a stone walkway. Given the quality of contemporary American letters, it might be tempting to be able to walk on one of our current authors (one engaging in minimal plagiarism).

The greed displayed by the ownership of professional sports is boundless. Major league baseball has considered the feasibility of placing advertising patches on the sleeves of uniforms. Many sports teams, with limited appeal, engage in the practice, but baseball has only used a special designation when major heroes die. Now, we may be exposed to Viagra, Preparation "H," Dr. Pepper, video games, and Victoria's Secret when the batter swings at a pitch.

From the fan's point of view, the patches would be difficult to read at a distance. More importantly, the home team's choice of advertising may offend the religious or moral sensitivities of the opposing pitcher and provoke a high, inside fastball. The only advertisement that would not create a negative reaction would be steroids. Incomprehensibly, major league baseball has not invoked a total ban on this genre of abuse.

In the final analysis, who would police the propriety of the patches? The Commissioner's Office, under the jurisdiction of some of the recent appointees, has been impotent, incompetent, and searching for club owner consensus before taking a definitive stand on any issue. To leave the choice to club owners, might mean that moral turpitude would be displayed on baseball uniforms.

The solution is to confine the message on the patches to a brief political announcement—a blank patch for Dubya's foreign policy might suffice as would a cigar for Bill Clinton's moral fiber. If the patches are placed on fencing uniforms, touché might assume a new meaning.

Honus Wagner was an All-Star shortstop for the Pittsburgh Pirates. He was selected for the Baseball Hall of Fame at Cooperstown. There have been few peers who played his position.

Honus, to honor his given name, reacted honestly and negatively to the smoking and chewing of tobacco. Rather than advocating his position privately, he expressed his opposition publicly.

Collecting baseball cards is not only an avocation, but it is also an obsession. If my mother had not thrown out my cherished collection when we moved to Washington, D.C., I would now be affluent.

The tobacco companies can recognize a potential devotee of their products, and they have subsidized the manufacturing of baseball cards. For many years, a virtual monopoly existed. The reverse of every baseball card included an advertisement for tobacco.

To punish Mr. Wagner for his virtue, the tobacco industry refused to create Honus Wagner baseball cards. As the price of vintage cards for distinguished players escalated (in excess of $400,000 per card), Honus Wagner cards are unavailable. In spite of the financial handicap, I can only assume that Mr. Wagner's progeny are proud but poor.

○ ○ ○

In the introduction, I mentioned that an injury to my pitching arm precluded the possibility of playing baseball in the Washington Senators farm system. Since pitching was curtailed, it is fitting that my management potential in baseball also failed to materialize.

A generation ago, Lee MacPhail, the president of the American League, submitted my resume to the chairman of the Search Committee for the commissionership of baseball. Bowie Kuhn was not elected to a third seven-year term, and the search process seemed to be stymied. When I learned of Lee's support, I called him and requested a luncheon.

At luncheon, we discussed the elements of the commissioner's role, the relationship of the American and National League presidents, and a range of contemporary issues including drug abuse, expansion of the leagues, salary escalation, and the free-agent policy.

Based on his experience and commitment to the game, it was my belief that Lee would have made a superb replacement for Mr. Kuhn. Since Lee had been in baseball all of his professional life, and he was nearing 70, he informed me that he had withdrawn his name from consideration.

I was intrigued with the nomination and with Lee's support. Since I did not have the requisite experience in sports management, and since my future was related to higher education and foreign affairs, I suggested to Lee that my nomination should be withdrawn. Planning a career is a work of art rather than a scientific experiment.

○ ○ ○

Finally, a few words about softball might be pertinent. Kim Schlink was a seventeen-year-old pitcher for the Southeast Regional Vocational softball team in Groton, Connecticut. At the time of the Associated Press story, Kim had compiled a 5-3 record and had struck out eighty batters.

The release stated that Kim was five months pregnant. The complaints in Groton did not surface until she began to "show."

In order to play (Kim was unmarried), she secured the permission of her parents; the school authorities; her family doctor, and three physicians associated with the obstetrics and gynecology clinic in New London.

The news release generated local hysteria. There was no school edict preventing pregnant athletes from taking the field. A rival school forfeited a game with Kim on the mound. When Kim played, she wore a pad around her middle. There were not any subsequent news releases.

Three pertinent issues were ignored:

* The impact on fellow students of allowing Kim to play. Extracurricular participation in school is a privilege not a right. A basic moral code had been violated.
* The effect on teammates and opponents. All of the other softball combatants were bound to compensate for her temporary infirmity, which violates the spirit of the game. Catchers wear protective gear, but the rationale is slightly different.
* Kim was not allowed to bat. Since high school softball does not employ the designated hitter rule, an inappropriate exception was devised for Kim.

When the coach was first informed of the pregnancy, Kim should have been removed from the team. With that statement, I have offended every unmarried pregnant softball player in the United States and Cuba.

○ ○ ○

At a state park near Granby, Connecticut, I took my baseball arm out of mothballs and participated in a softball game. I caught and played center field.

For more than thirty years, I had not thrown a baseball or a softball. In fact, I had not played softball since I was a youngster, and I found the game less than stimulating. On this occasion, from center field, I made several throws to home plate in a high scoring game. The throws were acceptable, but my calcified elbow objected. Since I was the oldest bloke on the field, it was obvious that I would engage in an act of stupidity and throw the ball hard.

At the plate, I batted only once and sent an easy fly to right field. I had forgotten that I wore glasses, and by the time the ball reached the batter's box, it was a bit blurred.

Following the game, I chatted with Tom Gorman, a former National League baseball umpire who was hired to umpire the local softball game. We concentrated on discussing the "good old days" which included three major league teams in New York City; pitchers generally completing the games they started; the pitfalls of league expansion; a relatively "dead" ball, and the inevitable injuries of an earlier era.

Less than a month after the softball game, Tom Gorman died of a massive heart attack. At age fifty-eight, the most respected umpire in professional baseball was called out on strikes.

Football—The Gridiron

When Monday Night Football Replaces a National Political Convention, America Suffers the Penalty.

Midway through the third quarter, the unbelievable was happening. Columbia was leading Harvard 17-0. The new Columbia coach, wearing blue shorts and a blue tee-shirt prominently marked "coach," to identify the guilty, was in seventh heaven. In his first game, the fans at newly-remodeled Wien Stadium (it does not have the "ring" of Baker Field) were delirious. Imagine, the Lions were winning a football game and against the Crimson. In the next twenty-one minutes, Harvard scored seven touchdowns in seven consecutive possessions and won the game 49-17.

Obviously, the Columbia coach was crestfallen. Rather than maintaining private despair, he described his team to a congregation of sports writers as "Drug-addicted losers. Once adversity comes . . . They're right back in the sewer again."

If I had been the President of Columbia, the coach would have been wearing another tee-shirt on the Monday following the Harvard game. Once the statement was confirmed, and it was confirmed, the only option was dismissal.

What did happen? Committees were appointed. The coach was allowed to continue. Lawsuits were contemplated by the parents of the players, and Columbia continued to lose.

The Coach's comments were indefensible. The "win at all costs" philosophy must be expunged from college athletics and particularly at an Ivy League institution which is committed to academic excellence. If the football team were addicted to drugs, the coach might have provided counsel and referred the matter to duly-constituted authority.

A few years after the blue tee-shirt caper, several students at Columbia University expressed indignation when they were informed that eleven prospective football players had been admitted as freshmen with less than minimum requirements. After twenty-one consecutive losses, which blossomed into an intercollegiate record, Columbia secured a waiver from the Ivy League to increase the number of borderline students (predominantly Black) who could be recruited to play college football. Obviously, the final decision was made by Ivy League academic leaders who were concerned about maintaining Columbia in the Ivy League athletic ranks. The issue was not matriculation but exposing football players to a high quality education while still fielding a team.

As usual, the few college students who chose to pontificate on the public record were poorly informed and missed the mark. In the past, for the wrong reasons, they had advocated stock divestment and student involvement in faculty tenure decisions. Now, the maintenance of admission standards for football players was a limited target. Dropping football was a better solution.

In American higher education, including the Ivy League, victories on the gridiron lead to alumni contributions, not academic excellence per se. The Ivy League provides, for most of the students afforded the privilege, the most outstanding undergraduate education in the United States. If that quality is to be sustained, the record of the football team is irrelevant. If it wins a few of its games, the alumni should contribute, and additional *qualified* recruits, who are delighted to play football, will graduate from a college of distinction.

The only option is to convert intercollegiate athletics into community, rather than college-based, pursuits. Since that option will not be exercised in contemporary society, Columbia students should open their books rather than attacking the university leadership. In present circumstances, academic standards will be relaxed for some athletes.

Standards are comparative. The least academically qualified Columbia football players will be academically superior to the majority of students at the typical college. The caveat is that those entering to play football must meet minimal academic standards, or college football is in jeopardy.

By the way, where were the Columbia students when minorities were admitted, in significant numbers, under affirmative action quotas? The ground rules have changed, but all complex institutions in a free society tend to be exposed to constituency pressure, demonstrations, financial reality, and volatile societal norms. When football players were admitted, under special circumstances, Columbia was applying special academic standards. Both approaches are suspect.

○ ○ ○

For many years, at both private and public institutions, the salary of athletic coaches was pegged to regular academic teaching and administrative scales. That approach tended to relate athletic compensation to the academic teaching and research functions.

Nick Saban, the football coach at Michigan State University, departed to accept the same assignment at Louisiana State University. Since the academic levels of the two institutions are not comparable, compensation is the only differential point.

At LSU, Saban receives a salary of $1.2 million per annum compared to the paltry $700,000 he enjoyed at Michigan State. When advertising income is added to the Saban base salary, the gross income will be several times the annual compensation for a typical university president.

The basic values in American society are reflected in the disparity between teaching and coaching salaries in higher education. My case rests!

○ ○ ○

I think I have discovered the perfect solution to college football's dilemma. In every college football game, by contract, the home team must be guaranteed victory.

I am confident some devotees of college football will charge that my putative bitterness with the present imperfect system results from broken dreams.

The charge is true.

As a former player, and a former college president, my winning seasons have been limited. To win at home and to lose abroad may provide the missing ingredients: a stable emotional base and a bit of perspective.

With hundreds of college teams playing football every autumn Saturday, half will win (except for those unmentionable ties). Under my proposal, the winning half will be the logical and deserving half—the host college. Think of the profound implications.

With impunity, host college presidents can invite distinguished alumni, governors, legislators, potential donors and even the players' parents to any home game. Post-game victory celebrations can be preordained. Positive vibes will prevail on campus. Additional contributions will be volunteered to preserve academic quality. Every Monday following a game, the mail of the host-college president will be friendly, substantive and germane.

In a period of financial retrenchment, scarce dollars will be preserved. Marginal players will not accompany the visiting teams. Scouting expenses will be curtailed. Recruiting will become an anachronism. Pre-game media reports will avoid emotional trivia.

Players on both teams will strive for individual perfection rather than team victory. Individual statistics will determine qualification for professional football and, with effective coaching and exemplary teamwork, the potential of personal attainment will be enhanced.

More and more alumni will attend home games to enjoy the star's quest for glory and to bask in the aura of "victory." Callow behavior, including the tarring and feathering of officials and player and fan fisticuffs, will be relegated to the history books. Pride will replace mayhem as the predominant motivation.

With professional scouts in attendance, outstanding effort will be nurtured. In rare cases, a limited two-platoon system will be re-instituted to allow a few players to enjoy both facets of the game.

Unnecessary roughness will be considered a criminal or civil offense because the only motivation for such nefarious behavior would be to limit the injured player's future livelihood rather than to insure victory for the cause. The courts will provide the remedy.

Football coaches will be evaluated on coaching ability rather than on the percentage of victories. Schedules will be arranged with colleges of comparable academic persuasion or to strengthen regional ties.

Readers of little faith may suggest that without the threat of defeat, football players will fail to give total effort. On the contrary, with professional scouts watching, every successful block will constitute a step toward a career. Win or lose—and a 50 percent record is adequate—each play will constitute an opportunity for personal growth.

Winning teams produce more professional prospects because defeat minimizes incentive. A premium player on a losing team is hard-pressed to rise to the occasion. Under my enlightened new system, a superb player on a mediocre team will always aspire, and his distinctive capabilities will be recognized. Personal incentive will replace team incentive.

Can any other mechanism be devised to allow owners of professional teams, alumni, college presidents and college football players a chance to share, however briefly, common objectives?

Winning isn't everything. It's the only thing—at home.

○ ○ ○

American sports culture is becoming more committed to the "fitting in" syndrome.

In training camp, the New York Giants professional football team adopted a reputed exercise in democracy. Each member of the team was required to have an identical room in the dormitory and to register at the dormitory. The coach opined "that no one is above the team," and that the egalitarian room arrangements facilitated a positive spirit, team rapport, sterling performance, and a desire to win. Unfortunately, this equality doctrine has not led to victory on the gridiron.

Allowing individual lifestyle preferences to surface in sports it not a negative concept. Cal Ripkin of the Baltimore Orioles always stayed in a hotel where other team members were not registered. Mr. Ripkin was a unique team leader.

Variable lifestyles can nurture team solidarity. If the coach leads his team in constant prayer, the results may be spotty. Unfortunately, most coaches are endorsing the practice. Even God may recognize that a few teams will lose.

The person with wealth, power, position and/or talent normally commands the trappings of office. There is nothing wrong with being different or living in a different style. In fact, envy rather than group solidarity may inspire superior performance. If you merely "fit in," you may emerge as just "one of the boys (or girls)."

In a recent article in the sports pages of *The New York Times*, Gerald Eskenazi, who is from New Jersey, took credit for a special piece which alleged that the members of the New York Giants professional football team were packing their "effluvia" in preparation for a trip.

There are a considerable number of sportswriters who release effluvia in their columns and a good many sports figures who resort to effluvia in describing their athletic ability, or the limitations of others. I have never heard of football players filling their suitcases with it to take to away games.

You can accuse the opposing team of being full of it or the opposing coach of utilizing it in his speech pattern, but the fortunes of the New York Giants are at a nadir if the players have to tote noxious vapors in their suitcases.

Do you think that the scribe meant "impedimenta"?

○ ○ ○

For two generations, I followed the plight of the Washington Redskins professional football team. With a few notable exceptions, the joys of winning in those years were limited. On January 30, 1983, the Redskins defeated the Miami Dolphins in Super Bowl XVII. As an indication of my growing maturity, I missed the first half. When the deciding touchdown occurred, my emotional outburst was confined to the breaking of crystal.

Our nation's capital exploded with childish enthusiasm. Federal civil servants were excused from work, a tribute which the death of Martin Luther King did not provoke. On the "Hill," Democrats and Republicans were embracing each other and broad smiles replaced frowns.

In a nuclear world with increasingly complex global issues with which to contend, it is less than reassuring that the situs of world leadership is prone to such inane frivolity. The United States is having a difficult time devising a viable foreign policy, but we are capable of cherishing a rare professional football victory in the corridors of power.

○ ○ ○

Although American football bears a passing resemblance to rugby, it has evolved as a distinctive American sport. Until the beginning of the twentieth century, it was an up-the-middle and "a cloud of dust" game. There was no forward pass until Knute Rockne, with Gus Dorais as the passer, humbled Army for Notre Dame in 1913. Since Army's decisive defeat, the forward pass has revolutionized football. Running into the center of the line became only one of many approaches to the game. The passer, pass receiver, and swift runner created a remarkable national following.

In contrast to the typical football fan, who applauds the superficial, the former player appreciates the limited nuances. Injuries can nip fond memories in the bud, and the height and weight differentials between linemen and backs present formidable inequities, but football has emerged as a grand sport.

With collegiate and professional football now covered in depth on television, and with the closeup of the action stressed, fans have developed an appreciation for the important options.

Baseball appeals to the dilettante (in the scientific sense) while football captivates the crowd with occasional strategy. John Madden, successful coach and broadcaster, and other football "scholars" are reducing the gap in understanding, but baseball is still the "national pastime."

Basketball—An Indigenous American Sport

Basketball may be the only major sport which was devised in the United States. The Director of the YMCA in Springfield, Massachusetts, developed the rules. In 1892, the first game was played. In 1896, the first college game was played in Iowa City.

The fundamental precept of basketball is that the players should not run with the ball. That rule has led to confusion and conflict. As a "non-contact" sport, the dribble, coupled with contact, have become the essence of the game. It is difficult for a play to be completed without the offensive player with the ball being pawed by the defense or by the offensive player charging.

Many of the rules of contact are ignored by the referees. For example, the distinction between charging and blocking is illusory at best and is certainly subjective. The "dunk" has become a mark of distinction rather than an irrelevance. As the players approach and reach seven feet, it is clear that the basket must be raised. Currently, there is only limited sentiment for this change. Basketball can be followed without recognizing the few complexities of the game.

During an interview, the coach of the University of Virginia women's basketball team stated that "my players are not cocky and glitzy. They are blue collar." That representative of academe should watch a few more television sitcoms. Blue collar America *is* cocky and glitzy. The Virginia coach has not seen many professional basketball games. Virtually all the male stars are "cocky and glitzy" but decidedly "blue collar." Why could not our Virginia representative of the coaching ranks say that her players were down-to-earth, likable people who deplore the slam dunk, trash talk, and the high five. If entertainers, of all species, were any more glitzy, there would not be any time to perform.

In contrast to the women in Virginia intercollegiate basketball, the men in the large universities, predominantly public, are blue collar, cocky and glitzy, not driven by moral principle, seldom graduate, and constitute a direct farm system for the professional ranks. At the professional level, with increasing recognition that a few high school superstars can move directly to the professional ranks, the college players who enter from the farm system reflect a preoccupation with compensation, minimal courtesy, and a generous portion of hubris. If the present trend continues, the next generation of professional basketball players (men) will emerge directly from outdoor, urban, unaffiliated basketball courts (grade school graduation might be a prerequisite). The ability to drop the ball through the basket while standing on both heels is not necessarily related to collegiate academic standards.

Don Issel, the former coach of the Denver Nuggets professional basketball team responded to a local Hispanic fan after losing a game. The fan was abusive and profane. Issel retorted with a slur that is national and racial. When "Mexican" was introduced, and the designation was heard by others, Issel was in trouble. He was placed on probation for five days with corresponding loss of salary, and interest groups in Denver recommended termination.

Subsequently, Issel resigned. Only the coach has been reprimanded. The fan's indiscretion has been ignored.

Fans must refrain from abusive language that can be heard by players and coaches. If such actions occur outside the arena, the police might intervene. In a sports environment, only the fans have the privilege of engaging in verbal fisticuffs and physical signs which would be subject to reprimand if performed on the street.

At a professional football game, bottles were thrown at the referees from the stands. Several of the culprits were identified and were ordered to appear in court. If the bottles had been directed at the coaches and players, judicial remedy would probably be moot.

Fan physical violence is not different from fan verbal violence. In Denver, Coach Issel misbehaved. The Hispanic should also have been subjected to punitive action.

American society, in public forum, has been ignoring behavioral mores. Purchasing a ticket to attend a sports event does not provide immunity from general societal rules. Unless the "Mexican" from Denver is reprimanded, Don Issel's probation is only a partial remedy. After a lifetime of coaching, his resignation is significant.

○ ○ ○

Some pundit suggested that the colorful, former basketball star, Charles Barkley of the Phoenix Suns, should become politically active in his home state of Alabama and run for governor. Mr. Barkley's response to the idea was positive, but he said, "People tell me that I have too many skeletons in my closet."

The United States represents convoluted values. A partially-educated man in his thirties is convinced that he is eligible to serve as governor by ignoring the unspecified skeletons and such irrelevancies as education, competence, and experience. The governor of Alabama has not considered himself eligible to play in the National Basketball Association, but that less than tenable suggestion illustrates the point.

A basketball player's expertise is immediately visible. A governor could perform miserably in his role, but he might be elected president of the United States. Measuring success in a complex assignment, as opposed to a professional sport, is related to collective judgment.

In a democracy, the electorate should insist upon relevant qualifications for all political nominees. If candidates are unqualified, the system is in jeopardy. Mr. Barkley should confine his aspirations to the United States Senate where dribblers and foul shot artists appear to be in demand. Bill Bradley was elected in spite of the fact that he graduated from Princeton and was a Rhodes Scholar.

○ ○ ○

A few years ago, the University of Missouri basketball team defeated number one rated Kansas in overtime. The victory also removed Kansas from the undefeated ranks.

In triumph, the University of Missouri coach was asked for the secret of his success. His response: "It was either our eptness or their ineptness which allowed us to win."

The University of Missouri features one of the premium schools of journalism. Unfortunately, the basketball coach requires a basic course in English rather than journalism. With such errors, the coach is "ept" to ignore the matriculation requirements of his basketball recruits.

The University of Connecticut Women's basketball team defeated the University of Oklahoma to win the NCAA championship. This was UCONN's third women's title in eight years and the second undefeated season. Their record was 39-0, and the five members of the starting team were selected as All-Americans.

The coach, Gino Auriemma, discharging his first college role in that capacity, manifests a unique ability to induce his teams to play with precision and teamwork. With the record that has been amassed at the University of Connecticut, his players have tended to ignore his volatile temperament and to concentrate on his instructional qualities.

In spite of the current sentiment of women coaches which tends to disparage the role of men as coaches of women's intercollegiate basketball teams, women's basketball depicts a few positive traits in the collegiate ranks. Virtually all the women college players graduate on schedule. The selfless passing and excellent shooting have created a game which is a pleasure to watch. The demeanor of the players is exemplary.

Thirty years ago, in its infancy, women's collegiate basketball was ignored. The shooting was gauche, and the quality of coaching was suspect. In 1972, NCAA Title IX, which created equality of opportunity for women's collegiate athletics was approved. The most immediate and fundamental change has been in basketball.

Today, three point and foul shots are almost professional. The players exhibit strength, speed, solid teamwork, and a commitment to the game. In a few years, the fans and the commercials will change the ground rules. In the meantime, women's college basketball is a legitimate and satisfying sport.

By the way, the University of Connecticut Huskies won the Women's NCAA championship again last year.

Track and Jogging

Are runners born strange, or does practice accentuate the trait?

When I was in ninth grade, I started running. Because my genes produced natural speed, I gravitated toward the dashes. I ran in college varsity competitions until I graduated.

In the military service, after returning from Korea, there was time for golf, tennis, and baseball, and there was not any inclination to run. Beginning my employment career in Washington, D.C., I developed a habit of running late in the evening. Since a "dash" was no longer feasible on suburban concrete, running a bit further became a viable option. With each passing year, the speed was reduced; the distance increased, and I conjured up mental gymnastics to occupy the time. For example, if I could complete "x" distance, "y" good would accrue to my benefit.

After a half century of running, I cannot correlate good fortune with any milestone. The only positive note, other than physical conditioning, is that I am still running. Track is a team sport, but acutely introspective. There are moments of joy, but in contrast to other team sports, it appears to be easier to write about personal running experiences rather than emphasizing the impact of society on the sport or the changing objectives and mores of the players and the fans. Track is basically a personal commitment. Even when participating with a team, the consequence of a victory or loss is limited when compared with the personal relevance to the track participant.

Until my sophomore year at Cornell, I assumed that I would emphasize football and baseball for which I displayed some talent. Injuries denied continuing participation in both sports, and I concentrated on track.

In the spring of 1948, after injuring my left (pitching) elbow in baseball, I tried out for the varsity track team. I qualified for the 100, 220, and short relay (440 yards). In three years, I ran in a dozen meets and earned my varsity letter. Track was a "backup" that I enjoyed and that kept me in physical shape; however, it missed the greater challenge and camaraderie of team sports for which I was prepared by talent and disposition.

The friends with whom I was associated on the Cornell track team were special and several became lifetime associates. Howie Acheson, a miler and a fraternity brother, became "best man" at my wedding. Bob Munsick was a fraternity roommate and a broad jumper. Al Longley was a grade school friend in Syracuse with whom I competed in junior high school in basketball and baseball, and who was also a fraternity brother and member of the Cornell track team. Norm Dawson was two years older, fraternity brother, and the fastest member of the track team. Nelson Schaenen, Jr., was a member of the track team and is still a close friend.

In 1950, in my senior year in college, there were four varsity members who received international recognition. Charlie Moore, who visited us at our home in St. Thomas in the US Virgin Islands, won the 440 yard hurdles in the 1952 Olympics. Bob Mealey placed in the half mile in the same Olympics. Walt Ashbaugh, a younger fraternity brother, took third in the Olympics hop, step, and jump.

Those associations were, and are, unique, but the most memorable experiences involved two of the very few Blacks who matriculated at Cornell immediately after World War II. Both were stars on the Cornell track team.

Paul Robeson, Jr., whose father was an All-American at Rutgers, was an engineer and a high jumper. We became friends and were seatmates on the flight to Detroit to compete against the University of Michigan track team.

In Ann Arbor, several members of the team entered a restaurant for a coke while waiting for the train to Ann Arbor. Paul and I were part of the group. The waiter refused to serve Paul, and I intervened. Unbelievably, gentle persuasion worked. I have never forgotten the sense of humiliation. To experience discrimination in a public place, in a large city in the middle west, was unanticipated.

A closer friend on the track team was Meredith ("Flash") Gourdine who was two years my junior and who won a silver medal in the broad jump in the 1952 Olympics. Several times per week, Flash and I would work on our "starts" at the outdoor track after dark before completing the daily workout.

Flash graduated near the top of his class in the demanding field of engineering physics. He was an officer in the US Navy and completed the doctoral program at California Institute of Technology. He became the chief executive officer of a technology corporation. As an inventor, he patented the first successful defogging system for airports.

On several occasions, we met in New York City. Only a few years after graduation, Flash began to lose his eyesight. Subsequently, the condition was diagnosed as diabetes. In his mid-forties, he became virtually blind, lost a leg, and was confined to a wheelchair for the rest of his life. Flash continued to devise patents on the West Coast, and he died in 1998.

Following college, I made friends with two other former Black track participants. In 1960, Rafer Johnson was the Olympic decathlon winner. In 1962, Sargent Shriver recruited him from the movie industry in Los Angeles. In the early days of the Peace Corps, Rafer and I worked at the Peace Corps in Washington, D.C. During his brief stay in Washington, we became friends, and track was the point of departure.

A few years later, while I was serving in Kenya, Mal Whitfield, the 880 meter champion in the 1948 and 1952 Olympics, was regional sports officer with the United States Information Center in Nairobi. He was an excellent teacher and coach. His book, *Learning to Run*, inspired many of the early African runners, particularly the successful long-distance runners on the Kenya national team. Mal won five Olympic medals, three of them gold, in London in 1948 and in Helsinki in 1952.

The Last Competitive Race

In August 1982, while running in Central Park in New York City in late afternoon, crowds began to assemble on the main roads. Since I was running at a snail's pace, I realized that they had not made the trek to Central Park to observe my style. Without realizing it, I was ushering in the annual three and one-half mile Challenge Run which was sponsored by a major bank.

There were three separate races combined in a single effort. Men who averaged under seven minutes per mile were allowed to start in the front ranks. All women competed in the second "tranche." The final group was composed of the rest of the men who emulated my sterling accomplishments.

More than 3,000 runners participated. Although there were a few score who had been practicing regularly (Olympic and Marathon leading times), the great majority were young, weekend runners. A few of the women finished with the first group. The overwhelming majority, men and women, finished together. At the rear there was a generous percentage, a few of whom may still be running.

A year later, I ran in the Manufacturers Hanover Corporate Challenge Race in Central Park that I described previously as a running spectator. My colleagues at Lincoln Center insisted that I run. More than five hundred teams were entered from the profit and nonprofit corporate communities. In excess of 3,000 runners were once again in the race, including a contingent of six from Lincoln Center.

The Central Park course began at the Tavern on the Green restaurant, followed Park Drive East up a lengthy hill to East 90th Street at the Metropolitan Museum, doubled back to Park Drive West, and returned to the Tavern for the finish. The temperature was in excess of 90 degrees F., and the humidity was 85 percent.

As the race began, the "stars" went first followed by the women. I took off with the remaining thousands, and our movement was severely restricted on a narrow street. In the clog of runners, I noticed that I was at least twenty years older than virtually all of the others. Every corporate entity in New York City had combed the employee ranks to identify competent, youthful runners for the annual sacrifice. If the "in house" talent was not distinguished, many corporations recruited runners of national prominence who were placed on the payroll for a few weeks. The performing arts staff at Lincoln Center who sat behind desks all day, and attended performances most evenings, were relegated to "also-ran" designation. Devotees of the performing arts would have objected strongly if we had recruited outstanding runners from those who were practicing violin once per year.

After one-half mile, I felt drained from the humidity, limited sleep, and the hot concrete streets. I realized that the pace was much faster than my occasional weekend jogging. For the first mile, most of the runners were passing me. I did not imagine that most would drop out quickly. At the first turn, about halfway in the race, I was confronted with a profound lack of vitality. A noble citizen with a hose inspired a bit of pep as well as appreciation.

At the three-mile point, I realized that I was beginning to pass scores of runners. Although all of my muscles and nerve endings were advising me to stop, I decided that finishing was a point of honor for the performing arts in New York City. It finally occurred to me that my previous competitive track commitments had never exceeded a race of more than 220 yards. I was not physically or psychologically prepared for a race of three and one-half miles (28 times farther). I had never been timed for a mile, or clocked my jogging efforts, and I recognized that I was drained. I was unable to respond to the sprinter's instinct for the last one-half mile. I crossed the finish line (barely) in twenty-nine minutes and forty-two seconds (about eight and one-half minutes per mile). The first twenty runners were in the five-minute per mile range. My time placed me in the approximate middle of the slow pack. I assume that the corporations represented by the best runners were convinced that advertising paid dividends. Since I was the last runner from Lincoln Center to finish, my younger colleagues were friendly, but we did not win a prize.

As a result of this humbling experience, I have developed the deepest respect for the multitude who are able to finish marathons, and even three and one-half miles, in distinguished times. As usual, the weekend participant, in any extracurricular endeavor, should concentrate on conditioning, and a sense of well-being rather than a competitive rationale. For several months, it was necessary to stand at my desk.

Seeing Life Through Jogging

The greatest difficulty in jogging is getting ready.

An analysis of jogging in several countries demonstrates why the League of Nations never realized its potential.

In Munich, as I passed an elderly gentleman in the neighborhood park, I was treated like a foreigner with a particularly noxious social disease. In London, they expected me to either make, or listen to, a Hyde Park speech. In Den Hag, as I approached, lady joggers crossed to the other side of the street. In Copenhagen, where no other human being has jogged, I was treated like a celebrity. In Rome, my bottom was pinched with good spirits. In Paris, I was stoned, even the day after the night before. In Lisbon, my calves were always warm from the hot air generated by the near misses of wayward canines.

The Domestic Scene

In New York City, the carbon dioxide which I inhaled should induce President Bush to endorse the Kyoto Treaty. In Washington, D.C., I received slight, severe nods from Pentagon officers who would qualify for "skin head" affiliation. In New England, teenage drivers treated me like a moving target, and in New Mexico, I am chased by coyotes and large dogs. (Are they black bears?)

As a jogger ogles the tourists sipping Kir at the St. Moritz sidewalk café, he/she is scrutinized for evidence of idiocy or obesity and relegated to obscurity. Entering Central Park in New York City at Sixth Avenue, the significance of "The Avenue of the Americas" becomes clear. Simon Bolivar, "El Libertador," dominates the small plaza, and a dozen ornate, horse-drawn carriages were assembled for tourist enjoyment. The drivers with Irish brogues intact posed in top hats and tails, while the horses nuzzled the remnants of the noon meal, and the pedestrians attempted to dodge the remains of yesterday's comparable repast.

At that time, Central Park was undergoing major changes, and the results were intoxicating. After seven p.m., this section of the park was closed to motorists. From the floorboards of Manhattan, long-distance walkers emerged with their preternatural hips; the marathon runners invoked instant admiration, the jumble of joggers which included the heart patient, the teenage dilettante, the erstwhile Jets linebacker, and the proverbial little old lady in tennis shoes, also emerged.

Several of the joggers sported exotic tee-shirts which captured days of triumph (The Pt. Bustard Mixed Marathon) or years of glory (The University of Harvard, sic), or a fleeting moment of truth (Women Belong in the House...or the Senate). There is always one bloke who ruins the neighborhood (Moose Meat Makes Me Horny) or one esthete who leaves us cold with a mysterious acronym (PDRAC).

Daniel Webster's likeness provided a measure of sobriety; however, rollerskaters with undulating parts, gigantic knee pads, elaborate costumes, and earphones transmitting the latest musical irrelevance returned us dramatically to the diversity of "the Big Apple." Ambulance patrols searched for those who misjudged their talents, and police cars provided a forceful reminder that the melting pot does not always concoct a delectable stew.

Every evening, at approximately six-thirty, within a shout of Bolivar's statue, a grey-bearded gentleperson, named Adam Purple, could be found wearing purple running shoes, a purple bookkeeper's visor, purple shorts, and a psychedelic purple short-sleeved shirt. His mission, which he chose to accept, was to organize the oaten residue, shred it into a fine powder, direct it into a dustpan, and conserve it in a plastic (purple) shopping bag. Reputedly, Mr. Purple supplied organic material for his garden on the Lower East Side. Unfortunately, the omnipresent ambulance did not have bars on the windows.

Returning to the point of origin, a jogger's normal objective, it is clear that Central Park represents a microcosm of the best and the worst that a great city can offer.

○ ○ ○

In Washington, D.C., I ran from my downtown hotel to the US Capitol via the Mall and returned via the Washington monument.

As I left the hotel, it was raining gently. Within minutes, a fresh wind arose. As I approached the Air and Space Museum, on the south side of the Mall, the lightning was jousting around the Capitol dome, and the thunder was playing John Philip Sousa. There were not any other runners which should have sounded a warning. Unthinkingly, a few pedestrians were huddled under the trees. The puddles were so deep that my running was impeded.

For the first time running on the Mall, the absence of runners and walkers was electrifying (nature produced the real thing).

In the quiet dusk, it was a special privilege to admire the buildings and trees between the Capitol and the Washington Monument. In the rain, the Washington Monument was visible in the west, and at the Air and Space Museum, I was reminded that the Spirit of St. Louis was hanging prominently from the ceiling. The US Botanic Garden conjured up memories among the cacti. As usual, the Capitol was intriguing. I was reminded of several sessions of House and Senate Committees before which I testified. Heading west, I passed the National Gallery of Art, the Natural History Museum, and the Museum of American History. As a former long-term resident of the Washington metropolitan area, I felt that I was renewing intimate contact with old friends.

I decided to return to the hotel via the Ellipse and the White House. The memories were equally vivid. With the wind and rain in my face, it was difficult to keep moving. At the hotel, I shed my soaked clothes, took a refreshing shower, and thought fondly of the beauty and joy of our nation's Capital. With few exceptions, weather conditions should not preclude running.

○ ○ ○

After returning from Europe, for the first time in six years, I reintroduced a series of wind sprints at the conclusion of my evening jog. Without studying the evidence, I had assumed that sprints, at my age, were problematic. In fact, the sprints are probably more important than the jogging in order to facilitate proper circulation and other "good things."

As usual, we believe what is comforting, take solace in the easier approach, and fail to challenge our bodies while we continue to tax our minds. If Senator Proxmire continued to sprint when he was over 70, then I can certainly emulate the originator of the Golden Fleece Award for wasting taxpayer's dollars. After all, one man's sprint is another man's jog.

○ ○ ○

After three years residing in France, we returned to our home at the shore in Rhode Island where we had retained our permanent residence for a quarter of a century. Now that age is exacerbated by cold weather, our thoughts centered on warmer climes. In leaving France, I began my retirement, and our priorities centered immediately on finding a refuge where the birds and the climate were exemplary.

St. Thomas in the US Virgin Island was our first choice. After a lengthy December visit exploring possibilities, we purchased a remarkable home that was owned by a colleague in the Council of American Ambassadors. The property overlooking the Charlotte Amalie harbor was unique and incorporated two houses and a cottage, a swimming pool, and a tennis court. A few months prior to our trip, a hurricane had resulted in considerable damage to the structures (and the pool and court), and we were able to purchase the premises for a reasonable amount.

For nine months, we worked every day restoring the property. In addition, my wife and I worked extensively on the grounds.

After a day serving as ad hoc contractor and yard hand, I turned to jogging. Unfortunately, we lived near the top of a significant hill. At the bottom of the hill, the city and bumper to bumper traffic prevailed; therefore, I ran around an abandoned hotel in our area which was damaged and vacant.

The temperature prior to dusk was acceptable, and I began my jog. The tropical plants and birds begged for attention. Unfortunately, the small hills which were an integral part of our large "hill" were more demanding than I anticipated. After several jogs, limited to a few miles each, I abandoned the practice and relied upon the exercise associated with preparing our home for habitation. I know why I never saw another jogger on St. Thomas.

After two years in St. Thomas, and a quarter of a century in Rhode Island (including stints overseas in France and Germany), we discarded our lifetime commitment to the Northeast and retired to Santa Fe, New Mexico. The changes were remarkable and enticing. This small western town is also the state capital. The art community is one of the most impressive in the country. The performing arts are exemplary and include opera, stage, symphony, chamber music, chorale, and ballet. The restaurants are excellent; the library is adequate; the costs are excessive; the scenery is intriguing, and the people are friendly and diverse.

My first jogging effort in Santa Fe was rewarding. In our residential area, there are only dirt roads. There is limited traffic, and the predominance of the juniper and mesquite that thrive in arid conditions have gradually become attractive. On the run, I was able to observe the Sangre de Cristo mountains above the city to the east, the Ortiz and

Sandia mountains to the south, and the Jemez in the west. The adobe houses which monopolize the area are amazingly attractive and reflect architectural diversity.

After two generations of running on pavement, and developing arthritic responses, it was relaxing to rely on the dirt roads. An occasional small rock presented an obstacle, but the roads are scraped and generally smooth. A detour on the arroyo of a dry riverbed presented a challenge. The sand is deep, but the aerobic impact is reassuring. The evidence of riding horses, and beer drinkers, adds a less than esthetic component. Avian friends are reluctant to be seen or heard in the aridity. The views are stark and beautiful for an import who has not lived in the west for fifty years (US Air Force in Idaho).

The heat in the summer, and the cold in the winter, limit the jogging options. On the other hand, without a lawn to mow, I am making the supreme effort.

International Exposure

In Kenya, the Ambassador's residence was located in Muthaiga, a northern suburb replete with British-style gardens. Our back lawn was large and included a swimming pool at one corner. We invited the members of the American Mission to be swimming guests twice weekly, but on two or three of the remaining days, I jogged barefoot around the lawn's circumference. Even in hot weather, at more than 5,000 feet, the conditions were perfect for running. I admired the innumerable varieties of tropical trees and flowers at the Equator, and 1,500 species of birds in a country the size of Oregon provided a fair sample at the Residence. I will never forget the distinctive call of the Red-Chested Cuckoo, the "rain bird," which is heard frequently but seen infrequently. The "wip, wip, weeoo" descending notes can be roughly translated as "it will rain."

Our children, Bruce, Sherry, and Scott (ages twelve, ten, and eight) in the late 1960s, participated in the Fergolympics, that incorporated running and swimming events. Their commitment to running has lasted for a lifetime. The fond memories of Kenya include the late afternoon events at home in Nairobi.

For more than two generations, Kenyan men (and increasingly, women) have dominated international long-distance running. The United States Information Service in Nairobi provided essential support for the development of middle and long-distance runners. Kipchoge Keino was one of the most distinguished victorious Kenyans.

After a gap of a few years, Kenyan runners are back in the news. Running camps have been established in the western highlands. At 9,605 feet, the camp in Kapsait is an excellent example. Many of Kenya's long-distance runners train at Kapsait.

The definition of "camp" is basic. There is not any electricity or running water, and the starch meals are not exemplary. A generous number of outstanding runners have delivered victories in the New York, Boston, Los Angeles, Honolulu, Sao Paulo, Paris, Amsterdam, and Milan marathons. They run on dirt paths in the high elevation dense forest. The altitude, trainers, and basic talent are the magic ingredients.

The camps are minimally supported by sporting goods corporations which provide airline tickets and related expenses in exchange for the runners wearing their logo. That approach is being supplemented by the plan to include paying "tourist" runners at the camps. Upgrading the quality of the camps will be a major undertaking. Tourists will not be attracted by communal outhouses sporting the requisite "holes" at ground level.

If corporations are recruited to improve the facilities, the quality of Kenyan runners will be in jeopardy. The amateur "tourist" runners will command the attention of the Kenyan runners. The amateurs from relatively affluent countries would contribute significantly for the privilege of camp attendance. The Kenyan runners would be distracted by western goods and values. The preoccupation with running would be replaced by the "good life."

Upgrading the camps to secure profit from amateur runners may provoke a negative impact on Kenyan excellence in long-distance running.

O O O

During our Peace Corps assignment in Thailand, the front yard in Bangkok served a comparable purpose. The lawn was long and narrow, and I resorted to a routine that was appropriate for the ambience. I threw a football the length of the lawn and retrieved it with a semi-sprint. Thirty minutes of that routine several times a week was the only exercise I could capture. While visiting the volunteers in the provinces, exercise was confined to extensive walks in the villages.

O O O

My frequent arrivals at Heathrow Airport in England were followed by the always unique, and supremely comfortable, cab ride to the hotel. London cabs make you feel that your destination, and time of arrival, are unimportant.

After a few hours of "jet lag" sleep, I unpacked my running togs and jogged in Hyde Park. In a variety of ways, Hyde Park provides the most enjoyable ambience in which to run. The number of walks is infinite, the size and diversity of plots preclude boredom, the permanent buildings and statues are historically and esthetically exciting, and the evolving panorama of people is endlessly stimulating. Twenty years ago, the human sights were confined to an occasional jogger and a few little old English ladies, in proper attire, being led by long-haired effeminate dogs.

Today, in contrast, there are scores of Arab women entombed in black, with Purdah veils, chattering like magpies in claustrophobic islands of humanity; a gaggle of Chinese school girls freeing caged birds to garner ultimate grace from the revered Tao deities; groups of Indian youths playing football (soccer) in minuscule grassy fields; a myriad of runners emulating mice in a maze; West African visitors ogling the British "birds"; and a profusion of nationalities punting amicably, but in separate worlds, on the Serpentine water hole which divides Kensington Garden from Hyde Park.

Lawn chairs, provided by the city fathers, are used and not abused. Every evening, a miracle occurs when the chairs remain in the park rather than being transferred to private ownership.

The gardens behind the Albert Memorial display a profusion of expertly blended colors including rare bushes and small trees which for some reason, probably community pride, remain committed to the public weal.

The bandstand in Kensington Garden invites a return visit. The Albert Memorial, although excessively ornate, dominates the western border of the park and represents the epitome of queenly love as well as the architectural hyperbole of an era.

On a remote path north of the Serpentine, a statue commemorating John Speke, the British explorer, illustrates the British proclivity for understatement: "Speke-1864-Victoria Nyanza and the Nile." The horse and the rider statue, depicting "Physical Energy," induces immediate countermoves to avoid imagined thundering hooves. As you leave the Park at Hyde Park Gate, Lord Byron's introspective demeanor conjures up memories of Greek battles lost and Italian hearts broken.

The victory lap features a return visit to the Marble Arch. The speaking voices are silent until the next morning when the critical, and uncritical, issues of our day will be offered to Sunday audiences ranging from the speaker to hundreds of avid listeners mesmerized by dementia, articulateness, relevance, or merely transfixed by curiosity.

As an inveterate traveler, with a waistline to match my culinary inclinations, jogging has become a way of life. With twenty countries under my belt, literally, I am now preparing a fascinating article: "Jogging and Jingoism" which is a sequel to "Dog Bites Around the World." My weight loss has been minimal, but my knowledge of history and canine identification has improved.

○ ○ ○

O O O

For four years, we lived in Munich, Germany. Our home was located in Bogenhausen which was only a mile from Radio Free Europe/ Radio Liberty where I was employed. The hours at the Radios were long and constant, and I resorted to jogging late at night in a park near our home.

The park was surrounded by trees. A wide walking path circled the park, and there were scores of flower beds in the interior. Late at night, there were no people or dogs. Of equal importance, security was not a problem.

The houses in the area were pre-World War II: tall and stately, stone, and extremely attractive. While running, I could admire the houses through the trees. In the spring and summer, the interior grass and flowers were stimulating. The classical streetlights provided sufficient illumination to watch the placement of my feet and the interior beauty of the small park.

After jogging and a shower, sleeping was not an issue. In spite of thirty trips to New York City and Washington during the four-year Munich assignment to attend Board meetings, my late runs provided essential exercise and a change of pace. In late evening, I never saw another runner.

O O O

For three years, we lived on the Left Bank of the Seine in Paris. Our apartment was located in the seventh *arrondissement* (district) a five-minute walk from my office at the American University of Paris on Avenue Bosquet. The area was unique. It afforded a marvelous identification with Paris including small, distinctive restaurants, a grand farmer's market on Rue Cler, a unique introduction to history, vintage buildings, a remarkable access to downtown Paris on both sides of the River, and friendly, interesting denizens who were only dimly related to the elite who patronized the Avenue des Champs-Elysees.

During our residency in Paris, I took every opportunity in the evening to run in the area near our apartment. For the first year, I concentrated on the Parc du Champ-de-Mars which was southwest of our apartment. In the park, a broad outer pathway surrounded exquisite gardens. The Eiffel Tower commanded the north end. Initially, I concentrated on the beauty of the Eiffel Tower, the gardens, and the lovely stone houses on both sides of the park.

Without minimizing the continuing appeal of the tower, et al., the Ecole Militaire, at the southern end of the park, drew my attention. It was constructed in 1769 and is used by the military college. Because I had the privilege of seeing the building in the early evening with variable sun displays, and admiring the architectural lines every lap around the Champ, it is one of my favorite buildings in Paris. For centuries the military elite were trained in the Ecole, and the Champ served as the parade ground. During the French Revolution, the parade ground was the situs for two gigantic rallies, and for half a century it was the locus for world fairs.

On August 30, 1993, at the Champ, we listened with 100,000 other devotees to the lyric tenor, Luciano Pavarotti, perform a potpourri of opera excerpts which were disconcerting, short, and unpleasant including Verdi, Rossini, Bizet, and Puccini. At 58 years of age, his voice was assisted by overpowering electronic equipment. His image was projected on several large television screens. After hearing Pavarotti perform at Lincoln Center ten years earlier, the voice quality was disappointing; however, the evening ambience, the crowd, and my identification with the Champ de Mars were unforgettable.

During the last two years of our residency, I moved my aging jogging limbs east of our apartment to the Esplanade. It was not as large as the Champ-de-Mars, but it was wider, and there were more dirt paths to select for an evening run. The Esplanade is one of my favorite spots in Paris. On the north are the Quai D'Orsay and the Seine. On the west are beautiful private homes. On the east is the Ministry of Foreign Affairs. On the south is the unbelievably beautiful Hotel des Invalides which was constructed in 1671 to shelter 7,000 elderly or invalided military veterans. Les Invalides includes Napoleon's Tomb and the Army Museum.

Running in the evening, the views of Les Invalides were extraordinary. I realize that my repeated exposure to the facade was unusual, but the views were magnificent. In addition, at the northern end of the Esplanade, the Alexandre II bridge, one of the most exquisite in Paris, crosses the Seine.

If I had not enjoyed the privilege of jogging in the Esplanade and the Champ-de-Mars, other extraordinary structures might have emerged as favorites. My appreciation of Paris was enhanced by the opportunity to jog in one precise area.

○ ○ ○

As a defense against wild animals, prehistoric man developed running skills. Fast runners survived, and the speediest ran against each other for enjoyment.

In Greece, where youth was glorified, competitive track and field events evolved. In the Dark Ages, Greek and Roman track competitions were discontinued. Many centuries intervened before track events were resurrected in the nineteenth century.

In 1871, competitive running was instituted in New York City. Five years later, national track and field events were sponsored and have occurred annually.

In 1896, the Olympic Games were revived. As men and women have improved their conditioning through selected foods and precise training, the records for individual events have improved appreciably.

Because of my affinity for records, I have retained daily personal athletic data for a half century. Unfortunately, because of a number of major career moves, the early personal records have disappeared. The last thirty-three years of daily records have survived. I assigned arbitrary points to a number of exercises and sports, and I have prepared monthly and yearly summaries. A one-mile run was worth forty points, pushups and sit-ups warranted the same number of points as the number completed, and sports such as swimming were assigned points for finished laps.

Why is this idiotic bookkeeping exercise useful? First, it creates incentive for a sustained level of physical effort. Secondly, it represents a competitive spark in the quest for records. Thirdly, it satisfies the unrequited statistical pangs of a student who enjoyed mathematics and accounting. Fourthly, since I do not possess bond coupons to clip, I enjoy a comparable chore. Finally, in spite of the fact that the annual exercise total is slipping substantially, the record keeping is fun.

3

Minor Sports

Tennis

The derivation of tennis is unknown. More correctly, it is totally confusing. Scores of games were, and are, based upon the use of some form of racquet or hand and ball. Historically, the closest relative is "Le Paume" which was an indoor game originating in France. In the fourteenth century, "Le Paume" entered England, and, for some unknown reason, became "tennis" which was a perversion of French.

Until the nineteenth century, variable courts, with variable rules, rackets, and balls, were introduced in England and France in profusion. At the beginning of that century, because of extensive gambling and "fixed" games, the courts disappeared in both countries. "Lawn tennis," which is related to the current version, was introduced in England in 1873 and was played outdoors exclusively. Subsequently, lawn tennis was also played on an indoor surface. Although the origin is obscure, the word "love" is used for "zero" in tennis.

In 1881, the US Lawn Tennis Association was launched. For almost one-half century, it was exclusively for amateurs. In 1926, professional lawn tennis was accepted. Since that date, tennis, as we know it, has been a popular sport for men and women of all ages. The only vital change is player and fan demeanor. Following World War II, gentlemen and ladies were replaced by less urbane players. Amateurs trained to become professionals, and professionals have become preoccupied with money.

○ ○ ○

Twenty years ago, the National Tennis Center replaced Forest Hills in the New York region. Forest Hills appealed to ladies and gentlemen. The National Tennis Center appeals to all of us.

The National Tennis Center is the situs for the US Open National Tennis Championship. A score of beautiful composition courts are arrayed around the "center court" stadium which seats 10,000 fans. A bevy of carnival-like services, ranging from delicatessens to purveyors of cotton-candy, are concentrated in ten acres. It attracts "the best tennis in the world" unless you happen to be addicted to Wimbledon or the French or Australian Opens.

Only two realities affect these idyllic surroundings adversely. First, the jet aircraft arrive and depart from Laguardia, every few seconds, at two hundred feet over the center court. Secondly, unruly citizens now constitute the genre of contemporary tennis fans. In tribute to the earlier shenanigans of Jimmy Connors (whom I observed in competition in Hartford, Connecticut)and the subsequent obscenities of John McEnroe, it is difficult to distinguish players from fans.

Tennis was a sport, with unique finesse, that attracted sensitive players and fans who behaved in a decorous manner. The sport has been converted into a sideshow that attracts rude characters on the court and in the stands.

When a professional tennis player berates the officials for exercising the discretionary role which they are trained to discharge to preserve the integrity of the sport, the discourteous fan syndrome is released; professional discipline is in jeopardy, and the match results depend more upon psychological warfare than tennis skill. If one of the indecently compensated professional tennis stars were removed summarily from the courts after the initial fit, tantrum, or obscenity binge, tennis might regain its status as a competitive sport. The current tennis fans would return to professional football where such behavior is equally offensive, but, generally, does not affect the outcome of the game.

In athletics, and in life, duly constituted authority must be respected. When authority is exercised, the issue is not rectitude but respect for the office. If the referee or umpire is not professionally competent, the management concerned with the sport, and the national organization controlling the officiating, are obligated to correct the deficiency.

The integrity of the rules, as interpreted by the officials, is the hallmark of athletic competition. To question the judgment of the officials, in tennis or in any other sport, while the competition is taking place, and to engage in ridiculous behavior in the process, makes it difficult to insure equity and dispassionate decision making. When Jennifer Capriati failed to honor her commitment to appear at an international Davis Cup competition in Africa, discipline should have been invoked for another ethical breach.

At the National Tennis Center, before a center court match began, we sat in the wooden bleachers at an adjoining court and watched an elder and a younger entrant warm up. I recognized the elder as Dick Savitt, a 1950 classmate at Cornell University, who was captain of the Cornell tennis team, NCAA and US Open Champion.

Retiring from competition in his prime, Dick became a Wall Street investment banker. He still competes, with distinction, in national seniors doubles events and "coaches" young professionals prior to their major matches.

○ ○ ○

A long tennis stroke from the summer "cottage" estates which were owned by affluent entrepreneurs from New York City, the National Lawn Tennis Hall of Fame and Tennis Museum is located on a relatively quiet side street in Newport, Rhode Island. The building reflects early nineteenth century wooden architecture, and the grass courts are beautifully placed in the atrium.

The Tennis Hall of Fame appears to reflect the tastes of the idle rich who dominated the sport for more than a century; however, the contemporary professionals who bring American mores to the court are anxious to be admitted to the Hall. The grandstand surrounds the courts on three sides, and the ambience is uniquely attractive.

The Baseball Hall of Fame at Cooperstown, New York, is not residing where the sport was launched, but the Tennis Hall of Fame in Newport reflects the heritage of the sport. Now, if the players and fans can regain that heritage, tennis will be enriched.

○ ○ ○

For the first time as an adult, I identified (partially) with a movie star. I have no idea whether she will be able to act (the current evaluation is negative), but she behaves like a grownup. She is beautiful, dresses discreetly, chooses her language with care, and appears to be able to separate her personal life from her cinematic career. Although her presence in *Grease* and *Cabaret* in New York City suggest caution, I am referring to the actress who deferred her quest for millions, and acquired a Princeton degree, before returning to the cinema, Ms. Brooke Shields.

A few years ago, the sport pages were filled with photographs of Ms. Shields and the tennis star, Andre Agassi, projecting their love affair. Mr. Agassi's demeanor on the courts is not exemplary. The stars of the two worlds married, and within a few years, divorced. Mr. Agassi tied the knot with former German tennis star, Steffi Graf. Ms. Shields has remarried and returned to the cinema and the stage.

○ ○ ○

When we resided in Nairobi, the American Deputy Chief of Mission was Wen Coote. Wen was a graduate of Wesleyan where he starred in soccer. He was a foreign service officer and an expert on Africa.

In addition to his other attributes, Wen was an excellent tennis and squash player. To provide a break from office routine, we would play a bit of tennis. Our tussles were spirited and our friendship blossomed.

The courts at the Nairobi Club, near our home, were superb. Many members of the Diplomatic Corps played tennis, and Wen and I enjoyed the competition. My game did not improve appreciably, but my general attitude responded. Tennis is a marvelous game which can be played intermittently.

O O O

Directly across the street from the Radio Free Europe/Radio Liberty headquarters in Munich, Germany, there was a private outdoor tennis club. The eight courts were composition, and a considerable number of my colleagues took advantage of the proximity to the Radios.

My secretary, Carolyn Ruprecht, and I played singles, approximately once per week. Other members of the staff and I played sporadically, but the matches with Carolyn were special. Her game was outstanding, and she won several of the Bavarian championships.

Carolyn's husband, Siegfried, was a tennis player of national caliber. Before his death in a tragic automobile accident, he served as captain of the Austrian national team. We played singles occasionally, and we were runners-up in the tennis Club doubles tournament. Obviously, I did not complement his expertise.

On a few occasions, I enjoyed tennis with an RFE/RL staff member named Karl Kopitzki who lost his left arm in World War II. In 1950, he decided to resume tennis with a major handicap. He was left-handed, and he was unable to throw the ball up for service without falling forward. In his late fifties, his game developed quickly. He soundly defeated several younger players including present company. His strengths were extraordinary: placement coupled with top spin, the ability to return every shot, and the opportunity to practice daily. I did better playing the club champion rather than Herr Kopitzki. I can assure you that sympathy was not a factor.

○ ○ ○

My Senegalese opponent, in spite of the fact that he was the resident professional at the Novotel Tennis Club in Dakar, should never be confused with Ivan Lendl. I also cheated by practicing for an hour before the match.

The festivities began with the visitor from Munich winning the toss and the first game with three consecutive aces. Each player won service until the match was 3-3 with spirited rallies.

Leading 40-30, his return of serve dribbled over the net, and before you could say Jacques Robiensone, it was 4-3 his favor. After the longest game on a very warm afternoon, he enjoyed a comfortable 5-3 lead.

Thirty years his senior, and winded, I thought of the Gipper at Notre Dame, not at the White House, and won my fourth game with a booming service ace. It was my opponent's serve, and at 40-40, my hard forehand was out by a replay call. Following my serve, I came to the net. I attempted a soft lob over his head. Voila! It was out by a scream. Game, set, and still Novotel, Senegal champion!

The moral of this meaningless match is evident. A successful lob over your opponent's head requires practice, and a solid serve will keep an average player in the set.

○ ○ ○

Before landing in Santa Fe, we returned to our permanent home in Rhode Island. I joined the local tennis club. The pro afforded two refresher lessons, after a long absence from the courts, and promptly arranged a match for me with an automobile dealer from a nearby town. I suggested to the pro that I might run out of steam quickly, and that it might be counterproductive to renew competition prematurely.

In spite of my reservations, the match occurred on schedule. The auto dealer played a solid game, but because of the strong serve, I was leading 5-3 in the first set. At that point, without provocation, my opponent started throwing his racquet and using profanity while ladies were playing in an adjacent court.

My opponent was an "old hand" at the club (but not in age). I wanted to walk off the court, but I was reluctant to create a further scene. I was upset by his demeanor. I merely "walked through" four games in a hurry and lost the set.

My reaction to athletic competition is complex. I play to win. Of greater importance, I play for the fun which includes companionship. On this occasion, my opponent violated "the code," and I was not willing to continue the competition. To grit my teeth, and to ignore his demeanor, implied that I accepted his behavior. When I failed to respond to the remaining games in the set, he knew my rationale without provoking a confrontation. If only that genre of player were detectable in advance.

In sports arenas, discourtesy and boorish behavior seem to rule the roost; however, I do not have to accept a challenge in that environment.

○ ○ ○

When I was a newcomer in the US Virgin Islands, I had not been introduced to the tennis set. Fortunately, the folks from whom we purchased the property left a ball machine behind.

Several times per week, I would attack our court with the ball machine as my adversary. By setting the appropriate dials, the machine allowed me to return a hard serve, to slam a lob at the net, or to hit a low return to the baseline. Although picking up the tennis balls was a chore, I found my opponent effective and courteous.

When I was able to make contact with the tennis crowd on St. Thomas, I missed the constancy of the machine. Matches were not cancelled, and the times were not subject to scheduling alteration. A tennis ball machine is a work of art and a friend. It also affords an opportunity to improve your game.

After arriving at our Santa Fe home, I unpacked my tennis racquet and headed for a lesson with the local club pro. She was excellent and was able to attack a few of my nefarious habits which had evolved during years of inactivity. I was astounded by the racquet prices, the fees for a lesson, the equipment improvements, and the crowds playing tennis. With the aid of a gentle brace, the "miner's" or "tennis" elbow did not intervene.

As a result of illness, and subsequent operations, I have not been able to return to the courts. The spirit has been willing, but age has become a factor.

Other Racquet Games

Since variations of strung racquets (and an incidental paddle) are infinite, I have been exposed to an impressive number of racquet sports.

As a "wee tad," I began with table tennis (nee "Ping Pong"). My father introduced me to the sport at our basement table. The game is played with a small, solid paddle and a lightweight, hollow ball. Doubles is possible, but for me, singles represented the challenge.

In subsequent years, it is amazing the myriad times I have played the game in private homes. The equipment is inexpensive; it is easy to learn, and a single point can be challenging. The tactics are limited (unless experts are involved). As a "game" diversion in a private home, table tennis is rewarding.

○ ○ ○

Played with a hard rubber ball, and a long, strung racquet, squash was introduced at the Harrow School in England in 1850. With the exception of Pakistan, where many of the champions resided, it is played indoors utilizing side and back walls. In Pakistan, the outdoor courts have an open ceiling. In the middle of the day, with the tropical sun beaming through the roof, the players are faced with the challenge of survival as well as victory.

I was introduced to squash at my Cornell fraternity house. The experts from prep schools were out of my league, but at midnight, after studying for several hours, the competition, coupled with speed and technique, were welcome.

At the University of Pittsburgh, I played with faculty and staff colleagues. In Kenya, I continued the practice, but I have not participated for an eon.

Squash requires stamina, skill, and speed. The side and back walls are diverting, and the ball can only hit the floor once. The front wall must be hit before the floor is again in play.

◯ ◯ ◯

Once you transcend the difficulty of using "racket" or "racquet" (both are acceptable), the fun has just begun. In most establishments which include squash courts, there are also larger courts which can be used for handball. "Paddle Racquets" is played on a handball court. The rules are the same; however, short, laminated rackets, and softer rubber balls are used. As we "mature," paddle rackets becomes more inviting as our velocity and stamina decline.

◯ ◯ ◯

The game of handball probably predated tennis. The rules are the same as squash. Outdoors, there is another version that can be played on a single wooden wall.

In handball, the ball (which is softer than the squash version) is hit with the palm of either hand. Fingerless gloves are usually worn, and there is a bit of extra padding in the palms. In spite of that precaution, the palms are constantly sore (unless you play three times per day and become calloused or impervious to pain).

◯ ◯ ◯

You may have guessed that racquet games appeal to rugged individualists in diverse climes and weather conditions.

Platform tennis is an excellent example. It is played on an outdoor wooden platform, particularly in the Northeastern United States. In 1928, the game was invented in the USA. It is acceptable year-round, and devotees prefer the winter season when they dress for the occasion.

The ball is sponge rubber, and a sawed-off laminated racquet is used. The layout and rules are comparable to tennis except only one serve is allowed (with a net in the middle of the court). The ball can be played off the wire sides and back wall.

Freezing is one of the fringe benefits of platform tennis, but the game is fun and challenging. To find a court requires an inordinate commitment.

The ambience for indoor racquet games can be frustrating. Courts are normally in short supply. The costs are excessive. The exercise is generally desirable, but the waiting may not be acceptable. The trappings of indoor and outdoor racquet games may exceed the joys of exercise.

The names of racquet games defy description. In different sections of the country, the names vary. In addition, the designations change frequently. Standard reference books illustrate the problem. Racquetball sounds like a worthwhile pursuit, but what is it?

○ ○ ○

Badminton requires unassigned space. Outdoor courts are seldom practical because of the wind factor. Indoor courts do not exist unless you play in a gym, and that means that basketball is in jeopardy.

Except for tennis, badminton is my favorite racquet game. The long, strung racquet resembles a squash weapon, but it is extremely light. The shuttlecock or "birdie" has feathers and a rubber base which, because of its weight, is inevitably heading for the ground or floor and can be hit with impunity. The feathers do not intervene. The "birdie" must not hit the ground.

Until the mid-eighteenth century, badminton was played almost exclusively in India. It was not introduced in the United States until the early twentieth century. The game demands speed and agility. The eccentric shuttlecock requires instantaneous response.

Unless you have played the game, you may assume that badminton is restricted to small children as a short-term diversion. In fact, the game requires unusual dexterity. It may be the best racquet game for conditioning. In Thailand, I had the privilege of playing regularly. The Chinese residents were superior players. Our neighbor who had an excellent outdoor court, protected from the wind, invited us to join his regular group for spirited competition.

In the United States, I seldom see references to badminton. In our diverse, complex culture, I am certain that badminton is being played, but the competitions seldom meet sports page criteria. Also, it is difficult for senior citizens, even if they discover other "mature" players, to discharge the agility requirement.

Water Sports (On and In)

Ice Hockey

If you consider the Zamboni a river in Africa, you are not a true hockey fan or geographer.

As youngsters in Syracuse, my best friend and I used to hike through the woods for two miles in deep snow and frigid temperatures to play hockey on a farmer's pond. There was usually a foot or more of snow, and, before skating, it was essential to remove it from the pond with the shovel which we carted with us. When a significant area was cleared, it was necessary to remove our gloves in order to don the hockey skates. The temperature was usually 0 degrees to 15 degrees F., and the chill factor was a reminder of frostbite. The skating was superb. I remember vividly the glorious feeling of sending the puck past my friend who was guarding a makeshift goal composed of stones.

Hockey is a modern game which was invented in Canada. The province, city, year, and specific teams in the inauguration are in doubt. The year was approximately 1880, and the city was Halifax, Ottawa, or Kingston. Ice skating originated in Europe in the seventeenth century, but the facts pertaining to hockey are unknown or in dispute. In the United States, the first game of hockey was played in 1897.

In spite of the presence of a referee, two assistant referees, two umpires, and generous protective equipment for the players, professional hockey, as played in the United States and Canada, is needlessly aggressive. The sport has been compromised by infractions to the point where the game has deteriorated. The two-minute penalties apply only to a few of the myriad violations. Trapping, elbowing, spearing, high sticking, and charging are seldom seen or subject to penalties. A player can "check" another player legally to capture the puck or to impede his movement. Illegal checks are seldom detected.

Hockey is the fastest team game (thirty miles per hour on skates). The puck, which can be aimed in any direction, travels in excess of one hundred miles per hour. A baseball can erupt from the pitcher's mound at the same speed, but existing controls, other than deliberately aiming at the batter's head, generally suffice.

In international competition, the penalties pertaining to aggression are observed. The game is faster, saner, and more fun. For example, at the Salt Lake City Winter Olympics in January of 2002, international rules applied, and the games were exciting. Speed, deception, strategy, tactics, and a desire to win (fairly) prevailed.

If the same rules applied in the United States, there would be more hockey players, more devotees, and greater endorsement for a marvelous sport.

In my opinion, with the exception of baseball, hockey may be the most interesting, demanding, satisfying sport. The power play and the penalty shot illustrate two examples of the unique strategy and tactics which distinguish the sport. If offensive brute force, and the cavemen who practice it, could be subject to control, hockey would satisfy an extraordinary number of players and fans.

Swimming

My exposure to competitive swimming has been minuscule; therefore, I will confine my treatise to swimming for fun.

My parents built a shack overlooking South Lake near Gananoque, Ontario and the St. Lawrence River. The lake was three and one-half miles long with four islands. There were only a few cottages and a few tourists on the weekend. For many years, we were possessive about the lake and swam daily for several weeks in the summer. There was not any place to dive, and I engaged in long swims from island to island. Without the benefit of any instruction, I learned the basic strokes and concentrated on the side and breast strokes. If I had been taught, the crawl would have been the first priority. Rocks were omnipresent, and walking into the lake was essential.

As the youngest Boy Scout in the State of New York, I enjoyed scouting and earned twenty-six merit badges. As a Life Scout, I completed all of the required merit badges (except Life Saving) for the Eagle Scout designation. Because of my ear problems resulting from childhood disease, the medical profession frowned upon diving. I completed all of the requirements for Life Saving except surface diving to a depth of six to eight feet. With a medical excuse, the local scouting authorities still refused to substitute another requirement. It was suggested that I appeal to the New York State Boy Scout Council. The local refusal was upheld without a reason. I resigned from the Boy Scouts. To reflect my interest and skill in the water, I had completed merit badges in swimming, rowing, angling, and canoeing.

As an adult, my swimming has been erratic. Wherever we resided, I used the available sources including indoor and outdoor clubs, neighbor's pools, and large puddles. In the US Virgin Islands, our outdoor private pool was superb, and for two years I usually swam twice daily. At innumerable beaches worldwide, I fried my skin and enjoyed the salt water. Running in the sand at the water's edge was also a special treat.

In Rhode Island, the dream of a private pool became a reality. The old apple tree and a number of hedges disappeared in the lower backyard.

To curtail expenses, my spouse supervised the entire operation, subcontracting pieces of the action and deferring nonessential components. Upon completion, after the inevitable delays, we took our first swim. The ambience was beautiful: flowers, trees, birds, grass, views of our Tudor-style home, and thick hedges preserving privacy in all directions.

In spite of a basic heating unit, swimming was restricted to sixteen weeks in the year (June 1st through September 15th). In the year that we departed from Rhode Island, we swam on the 23rd of May. The water was stimulating and frigid.

One critical construction mistake was made. The experts failed to inform us that the shallow end of the pool must be deep enough to accommodate lap turns and sinking knees related to the breaststroke. No remedy was available. I found that it was preferable to turn before arriving at the shallow end. Filling the pool to the top, and cracking the rim tiles, created three extra inches which were inadequate to the task.

In St. Thomas and Rhode Island, I completed a prescribed number of breaststroke laps which was increased over the years. In Santa Fe, we swim occasionally at a local outdoor pool. Cavorting small children, and adults completing thousands of laps, serve as an effective brake on our enthusiasm.

Watercraft

Sailing has never been part of our heritage. At the camp in Canada, and on the salt pond in Rhode Island, we were confined to a Sunfish.

On one occasion, during a Labor Day weekend in Rhode Island, we joined friends at Newport to observe the final challenge round of the America's Cup race.

We boarded a magnificent sixty-foot power boat with a crew of four. The other guests included the dean of the Brown University School of Medicine, a manufacturer of parts for nuclear submarines, and the former owner of the leading radio station in Providence.

As we left the crowded marina on a beautiful clear day to join hundreds of pleasure craft, I recognized the idiocy of watching a renowned cup race. As the international participants tacked for position, we peered through the sails and smoke of pleasure craft to ascertain which yacht was in the lead. Since all observers must maintain a respectful distance, the combatants resembled colorful matchsticks flirting with the horizon.

In due course, we were informed that Australia II, sporting a new controversial keel, defeated the British entry to cap a 4-2 triumph which entitled Australia to challenge the American yacht in the final round.

Since the inception of the America's Cup more than a century ago, the United States entry successfully met the challenge every four years. In 1983, after the Americans had won the cup twenty-four consecutive times, Australia II was victorious. For a cup race, each competing vessel must be designed, constructed, and outfitted solely in the country it represents.

Watching the gross American tourist response, and reading the jingoistic drivel in the American press, I will never accept an invitation to watch another international yachting bout.

○ ○ ○

After rowing as a youngster in Canada, I completed the Canoeing Boy Scout Merit Badge and learned the important strokes including the diagonal draw, reverse sweep, back water, and bow stroke. Forty years later, because of the noise and maintenance of an outboard motor, we purchased a beautiful, handmade canoe for use at the camp in Canada. Unfortunately, our family Labrador Retriever decided to make a dramatic shift from one side to the other, and the canoe overturned. The only damage was to our field glasses, camera, and pride. We were able to retrieve the equipment from the bottom of the lake.

In Rhode Island, we purchased a manufactured canoe for use on the large salt pond. Because of our travel schedule, and the plethora of speedboats and jet skis on the pond, we seldom used the canoe. It was necessary to cross the main boat channels in order to reach the dunes and marshes (for water birds) which adjoined the ocean. Jet skiers seemed to treat the canoe as a target, and the wake was instantaneous and dangerous.

On the ocean side of the dunes, there was a three-mile beach with habitation confined to both ends (a breech-way and a small yacht club with access to the pond). At the yacht club end of the beach, there were designated swimming areas for residents on the pond. Beyond the breech-way, there were cottages for fishermen. At the extensive ocean beach in the middle, there were no buildings and only an occasional fisherman or swimmer.

Using the canoe for access, the beach was enjoyable, except for the jet skis on the pond. Gliding through the marshes in search of water birds was rewarding, and running on the wet sand reminded me of the early scenes in *Chariots of Fire*. Our canoe was the only one we saw on the extensive salt pond.

Over the years, we paddled along the pond littoral to have brunch at the quaint inn near the yacht club and to visit friends along the shore. As long as you refuse to give rides to large dogs with wanderlust, a canoe can be a blessing.

○ ○ ○

Although our elder son was a crew member in college, my exposure to rowing has been confined to pin row-locks in flat-bottomed boats. Since you cannot feather an oar with a pin row-lock, experts frown on the device. On the other hand, in rowing along the shore for plug fishing, a pin for the oar is useful.

Since the outboard motor for our rowboat at the camp was seldom in working order, it was usually necessary to row more than three miles to the end of the lake, and return. Since the lake was wide at the far end, I also rowed to desirable fishing spots and to remote locations for a swim. In Rhode Island, we used a Boston Whaler for lengthy water skiing outings.

Practice with an inferior rowing device is not a major hurdle. The stroke in a varsity crew is exposed to many more demands; however, my exposure to rowing a flat-bottomed boat has provided vivid memories.

○ ○ ○

As a boy, I considered fishing a delight. For hours, I would sit at the dock with my legs dangling in the water, and a worm, a product of my nocturnal efforts, dangling from the hook.

When I was a teenager, my father introduced me to the intricacies of plug casting. With a light bamboo rod, and a state of the art reel, I learned to place the floating plug in a calm spot near the shade of an overhanging tree. The distance and accuracy of the cast took precedence over the rationale for the kill. Although hooking a fighting small-mouth or large-mouth Black Bass was a challenge, I preferred the competition related to accuracy with a floating, wooden plug. I was an adult before I recognized that the dissection of a game fish introduced philosophical strictures.

As a father, I introduced my fledglings to the wonders of baiting a hook and watched with fascination as they reached advanced stages of angling maturity.

With one notable exception, I have not attempted to catch a fish for two generations. I spent a less than inspiring day landing a beautiful sailfish in the Indian Ocean off the Kenyan coast. At that time, I made a resolution to shun fishing. That pledge has not been broken.

In the intervening years, my deep concern for the ecology, including the plight of the fish and the waters in which they swim, has only been exceeded by negative reactions to the fishing clientele. I recognize that the fly-fishing coterie is different, but I have seldom been exposed to that genre. I have never seen a fisherperson, of the lake variety, with a pair of binoculars.

Now, in my dotage, I have retained my excellent left-handed fishing reel; however, my priority interest in the environment precludes its use. Although a few bodies of water have been improved, the general trend is discouraging. If you transcend the act of catching a fish, and the fishing clientele, the failure of conservation measures to preserve the ambience intervenes.

I admit that I enjoy fish cuisine; that the death of a fish, in my presence, does not represent a major ethical precept, and that I may discover a pond where the angling and power boating clientele do not predominate. In a world in which the moments of joy are restricted, I can envision the challenge of placing a wooden plug near a lily pad, but that plug would not have hooks. Until I am persuaded that the sensory organs of a fish are nonexistent, the hooks utilized in fishing represent a primitive way to die.

Golf

Golf is a grand sport. It requires consummate skill. Generally, the courses are beautiful. There are only a few minor hurdles.

In excess of three hours are required to complete an eighteen-hole round. If you play once per week, it is theoretically possible to maintain the quality of your game; however, once per week is marginal. If you play twice per week, ten hours should be allotted (including transportation, preparation, etc.). If you read, speak, write, take work home, nap, raise a family or garden, ten hours per week devoted to golf may constitute an inordinate amount of time.

In addition, the costs are increasing geometrically. Of greatest importance, if you play an acceptable game, and you attempt to adjust to the conditions just described, you play yourself, and the psychological impact is debilitating. A double bogey can ruin your day. Unless you live on a golf course, treat golf as a preoccupation, play professionally, or inherit a fortune, the time invested may not be warranted.

It is clear that golf evolved from field hockey. The game probably originated in Scotland. In 1860, the first tournament was played in England. In 1885, sustained interest developed in the United States.

In the USA, the sport spread rapidly. In 1935, there were 5,727 courses (compared to more than 3,000 in the rest of the world). Now, the number in the USA is astronomical.

It is tempting to make comparisons regarding the skill of individual champions and the quality of general performance. Innovations preclude comparison. For centuries, the ball had a leather cover and was stuffed with feathers. In 1902, a rubber cover was introduced, and virtually every year since, an internal weaving or material component has increased the velocity of the ball. Golf clubs have undergone major changes that have increased the distance and accuracy of the drive and irons. Only the lowly putter defies description.

When Tiger Woods won his third Master's title, and his seventh major, in the spring of 2002, the comparative evaluation of champions was renewed. Arnold Palmer (who is my age and whom I have followed for his entire career) was frequently mentioned. Jack Nicklaus, who is a bit younger, and won twenty-one major championships, did not win his seventh until he was 27 years of age, one year older than Tiger Woods.

At age 21, Tiger was the youngest to win the Master's. He won four consecutive major tournaments. He is exciting to watch and an inviting personality. Undoubtedly, he will establish additional meaningful records.

It takes years to establish a challenging record. Tiger should be compared to his peers not his progenitors. The sportswriters should restrict the hyperbole and confine their historic comparisons to the first golf course (St. Andrews, Scotland). Tiger Woods, a remarkable golfer and human being, warrants plaudits regarding performance but not premature predictions of eternal greatness.

○ ○ ○

Casey Martin, a professional golfer, has a rare circulatory condition which makes it difficult for him to walk. Extensive walking may provoke broken bones and even potential amputation.

Casey has the misfortune of being a superb golfer. He petitioned the Professional Golf Association to allow utilization of a golf cart while participating in PGA tournaments. The PGA rejected the plea. Mr. Martin sued the PGA under the terms of the Federal Americans with Disabilities Act which was enacted for different purposes. Several former professional golfers allege that the fatigue of walking eighteen or more holes per day is an integral part of the game of professional golf. I do not know how the PGA would react to bouncing a tennis ball before service, gripping the resin bag before a baseball pitch, or, heaven forbid, taking a practice swing in golf.

Obviously, every person cannot qualify for everything, but in the contemporary United States, we are making a noble effort. Women did not quite make it to the caves of Afghanistan, but an excellent golf swing, by a person of either gender, can lead to a university scholarship and/or a professional career.

If the PGA stipulated that Mr. Martin did not have to stroke any putt under ten feet, because of his physical infirmity, golfing standards would be in jeopardy. Mr. Martin should be allowed to ride a golf cart. He should be judged by the accuracy of his game rather than his method of transportation between shots on the fairway.

O O O

After a generational gap, on the spur of the moment, I once stopped at a driving range to hit a bucket of golf balls. It had been several years since I had swung a golf club. In the interim, among other things, I had contracted arthritis in my fingers and shoulders, and I was uncertain whether I could hold, much less swing, a club.

Selecting a dilapidated driver from the rack, I remembered my training. Reducing the club speed, the balls sped straight and true with considerable distance. Greed then intervened. In an effort to increase the distance, I increased the speed of the swing. Inevitably, the shots were wild. A few went further than previously, but a few were controlled by a slice that I had eliminated many years ago.

In senility, it is preferable to jog and rake leaves, with a light heart, than to hyperventilate with the intricacies of the golf swing.

Boxing

In New York City, I frequently relied upon the services of a bootblack at 42nd Street and Fifth Avenue. He was a former professional boxer. He was 40 years old (he looked 70), and his facial features reflected the impact of his previous profession.

In striking up a conversation, we concentrated invariably on the sport to which I had seldom been exposed. According to my friend, prizefighting is a noble profession in which every contest about which we read is "fixed." The decisions are predetermined by the promoters. Unless a fighter endorses the "fix" routine, he will be forced to change his line of work.

To illustrate his point, my informant alleged that Mohammed Ali, nee Cassius Clay, could never have defeated Floyd Patterson, and Sugar Ray Leonard could never have defeated Duran unless the "fix" were in vogue. In the boxing fraternity (I wonder if the sorority follows the same plan), it is clearly understood that there will be a propitious moment, in each major bout, for a "fall." Unless the outcome is preordained, a boxer with excellent technique could never emerge victorious over a "fighter." A person with "heart" could always triumph over a superb boxer.

If my shoes required a daily shine, I might have become a veritable boxing expert. On the other hand, if my friend was correct, he should have taken the prescribed "fall" before his face was subject to alteration.

A year later, I attended the closed-circuit television Hagler-Duran middleweight bout at Radio City Music Hall in New York City. The fight was preceded by a reception and dinner at "21" for the honored guests.

The bout was exciting. Few solid blows were landed by either boxer, and I could not detect which boxer was designated for the "fall." Duran confounded the experts by lasting the full fifteen rounds with style.

The animals were not present in the ring but in the Radio City Music Hall audience. Each distinguished guest paid a fortune (mine was complimentary) for the privilege of screaming for blood. Because only a small amount flowed, except for Hagler's left eye, there was uniform disappointment.

The spectators at a boxing match do not release aggression. They manufacture it. A cold shower would be more effective, less costly, and, judging from the aroma emanating from the hall, the benefits would be remarkable.

For the first time, I agree with Howard Cosell. Professional boxing should be outlawed. As a youngster, before the advent of television, I listened to the professional bouts on the radio. As usual, radio presented a "make believe" world. In the '30s, the Joe Louis heavyweight fights were magical. When Billy Conn's dexterity and footwork almost defeated the champ, the entire fight was "electric."

With the arrival of television, altering facial appearance intervened. The brutality and senselessness of the "sport" are manifest. Today, while a plenitude of governing groups designate their champions for each weight class (e.g., the World Boxing Council, the World Boxing Association, and the International Boxing Federation are the most powerful) distinctive criteria are applied to each weight class. Most of the intrigue of the sport has disappeared.

Archery

In the thirteenth century, William Tell, a legendary Swiss hero, defied public authority and was ordered to shoot an apple from his son's head with a bow and arrow. Every school child is exposed to the fable, and many artists have depicted the act. In 1804, Friedrich von Schiller wrote a major play in the name of our hero. Unfortunately, William Tell's existence has never been authenticated.

At the end of the fifteenth century, in Scotland, archery had become a compulsory national sport. As a concession to the dominance of the sport, the parliament banned golf as a threat to archery practice. Until the Spanish Armada in 1676, more humans were killed by arrows than any other culprit. At that time, the English switched to firearms; however, in North America, the Indians used the bow and arrow with devastating results until the end of the nineteenth century. Arrowheads have been discovered on every continent and accuracy evolved up to six hundred feet.

As a sport, archery was prevalent in the late seventeenth century. In the United States, the first archery championship was launched in 1879 and occurred every year subsequently except for World Wars I and II. The National Archery Association became the governing body and decreed that the bow should be six feet in length (less for women).

Until 1930, the sport was not popular. The Olympics incorporated archery as an event from 1900-1920, but it was not reintroduced until 1972. A new bow was authorized with a range of 850 yards, and the sighting equipment was improved appreciably. In the Olympics, the United States has been the leading nation in the men's events. In the women's events, South Korea has been dominant.

As a youngster, a friend introduced me to archery golf. My exposure was limited to one round of eighteen holes, and I was captivated. Without any formal instruction, I was able to use the bow and arrow without distinction.

The object was to shoot an arrow from the "tee" in the direction of the green and to shoot again from the place where the arrow landed until you penetrated the target on the green. For some experts, the scores were less than the average professional golfer.

Sixty years later, in the capital of Paro, Bhutan, we watched a group of archers participating in a contest. In Bhutan, archery is the national sport. The courses are twenty meters in length. The target is a thirty centimeter wooden slab placed in the ground. Although the distance to the target was not extensive, very few of the archers were able to hit the target on the first shot.

Bhutan competes in archery in the Olympics, but victories have been confined to regional meets. During two weeks in the provinces, we did not witness any youngsters practicing the sport.

Soccer

When a national sport is played with the head rather than the hands, collective thinking may be muddled.

Given my sustained interest in other team sports, I never participated in soccer or even kicked a ball until my sons, while we were living overseas, displayed a commitment.

In Kenya, as a member of the diplomatic corps, I played in a game against the Kenyan government (cabinet, permanent secretaries, and members of the parliament). Since I was selected as goalie, you can anticipate the outcome.

○ ○ ○

A few years ago, the Associated Press released research data concerning soccer which was compiled by the American Psychological Association. The data suggested that the repeated use of the head in soccer may retard selected mental functions. Repeating the exposure for several years may exacerbate the condition to the point where it emulates the fate of an interior football lineman or, more logically, a professional boxer. Several researchers are advocating the use of soft helmets. The "soccer moms" will undoubtedly repudiate the recommendation.

My aphorism overstates the case, but it is intriguing that several centuries elapsed before the negative impact of "headers" became an issue. In sports, the head is an asset but not as a battering ram.

○ ○ ○

In the United States, for several generations, soccer has enjoyed a small but devoted following. A half century ago, if colleges did not wish to participate in football, they fielded soccer teams. In the major colleges, soccer was fully competitive, but the interest, and the crowds, were limited.

During the past decade, the United States women's team was professional reigning champion; however, that attainment did not translate into paid customers at the stadia. Soccer has now overtaken track as the leading participation sport for women. Eighteen million youngsters play soccer. Seven million play regularly compared with five million who play baseball. In the last decade of the twentieth century, soccer was the only team sport enjoying a growth syndrome.

Soccer crowds are growing appreciably at the national level. The men's national team may attract 30,000 customers per game compared with 2,500 fifteen years ago. On the campus, the crowds are increasing but not fundamentally.

In Europe, the passion for soccer has led to aggressive behavior. In Italy, Great Britain, and Austria, collective emotion has produced major fan aggression. In Brazil and Argentina, the fans have demonstrated their collective unhappiness with negative results.

Given the trends in other major American sports, it is unlikely that soccer will fail to create aggressive reactions from the crowds. In sports, passion is related to publicity, the size of the audience, and a winning combination. In the United States, with winning teams and larger crowds, soccer fans will join the fray.

4

The Modern Olympics

The Summer Olympics

Courtesy of ABC-TV, I have learned more about gymnastics than I ever wanted to know. I have become hysterical as both genders have exceeded even their own expectations by winning a peck of games in the non-sport of volleyball. As I wait patiently for the track and field events to commence, which used to dominate the summer Olympics, I have been inundated with swimming events where another few laps, with the same stroke, qualified a teenager for another gold medal. Finally, I must cite the equestrian events where affluent people ride horses around a golf course, with a few hurdles, while dressed for virtually anything.

It is endlessly fascinating to witness the myriad ways men and women compete physically. The permutations of diversion appear to be infinite. With the "demonstration sports" of tennis and baseball destined for Olympic accreditation, precious medals may be awarded for tailgating, bridge conversation, lawn mowing, and my own specialty, watching the Olympics on television.

○ ○ ○

In covering the 1984 Summer Olympics in Los Angeles, ABC-TV was accused of every crime except distinguished coverage. In spite of the lack of distinction, I would like to award a trinket to ABC-TV for a thorough, fair, educational, and entertaining effort to discharge a public obligation that the other networks disdained.

The International Olympic Committee composed of defeated politicians, frustrated athletes, and the least common denominator from each country, without holding a hearing, collecting evidence, or waiting for the Olympics to end, opined that ABC-TV provided a pro-American bias, and that athletes from other countries had not received an equitable allocation of prime time.

ABC-TV is a commercial media organization located in the United States which insures coverage for the American viewer. In addition, the network has made a judicious effort to provide balanced international coverage; however, its primary responsibility is to feature the American Olympic participants.

As the distinguished IOC delegates sat in their Los Angeles hotel rooms absorbing the Olympic coverage that summer, they obviously ignored two salient facts: eighty million Americans were watching, and ABC-TV makes the pertinent footage available to each country. The appropriate jingoistic commentary can be appended.

Howard Cosell, who resided at the bottom rung of my hit parade of television commentators, presented the boxing events with candor and fairness. A few of the inexperienced former Olympians, who represented essential expertise re specific events, overreacted to the limited success of the United States' athletes; however, the coverage reflected natural exuberance.

ABC-TV has created a non-governmental medium, in the one country in the world, including Great Britain, where government control of the media has not generally become a debilitating factor. Because of the lack of control, when appropriate, ABC-TV has made negative comments about American athletes and Olympic policy.

The British decathlon champion, Daley Thompson, manifested a unique anachronistic perspective during the victory lap following his impressive demonstration. He donned a tee-shirt with a message expressing gratitude to Los Angeles and the USA for serving as gracious hosts for the summer Olympics.

In the women's 3,000 meters, Mary Decker from the United States fell after running into the barefoot Zola Budd from Great Britain (nee South Africa).

It is difficult to designate one of the runners as the culprit. Clearly, Budd had the lead of approximately one stride. Budd was too close to the inside lane. Decker ran into Budd. Decker fell and was out of the race. Budd saw her fall, lost her concentration, and was never in contention. Both runners may bear permanent psychological scars.

In a case of comparative negligence, Mary Decker should have been gracious. In fact, she was bitter, unfair, and nasty. In contrast, Budd attempted to apologize.

Neither runner will probably ever win the gold medal in the Olympics, but Ms. Budd deserves a citation. Through her post-race demeanor, Ms. Decker has permanently damaged her reputation. Of greater importance, the world has been exposed to an American athlete representing the stereotype which the citizens of many nations believe— arrogant, ungracious, and selfish. In Oregon, Ms. Decker may be a local heroine. In my book, she should investigate another profession.

For years, I have been writing and speaking about negative foreign perceptions of the United States. In the 1996 Atlanta Summer Olympics, the negative foreign reaction extended to the leading media.

At the height of a humid summer in a southern US city, the chickens came home to roost. Allegedly, the computer technology (invented in the USA) failed. The foreign (European) press had a ball debunking the myth that the United States is technologically advanced.

On a less elevated level, the quality of food was adjudged inferior, schedules were suspect, and transportation was considered unreliable.

Some of the comments were inane. "Good Chinese food is (generally) unavailable" which hampered the Chinese athlete's ability to compete; however, most of the comments were fair.

The most damaging blow was administered by *Le Monde*: "In megalomaniacal America," the Olympic games have been "handed over to private enterprise with the sole aim to make money."

President Clinton lauded Atlanta for an exemplary effort. The truth probably emerges between Bill Clinton and *Le Monde*.

The Winter Olympics

The Winter Olympics at Salt Lake City in 2002 were intriguing and well-managed. I have only one complaint. Efforts were made to convert the conventional, historic events into new, high-risk teenage-oriented events that were limited in duration, long on hype and meaningless virtuosity, and appeal almost exclusively to the marginally-mature crowd.

Recently, the winter Olympics introduced the "half-pipe" which imitates the roller-skating addiction through endless repetition of a deep half-circle on the inside of a large water pipe (in appearance). Moguls and aerials are featured which are only remotely derived from skiing. The recently introduced "skeleton" relies upon an ugly sled that is directly related to a cafeteria tray. More than a half-century ago, the "skeleton" was discarded as an event.

Short-track speed skating has also been adopted which includes an oval track about the size of a basketball court. It offers participants an unusual opportunity to batter each other for an advantageous position in abbreviated imitation of a race. "Short-track" provokes a plethora of accidents and infractions. Skill is hidden from view. In a few years, these new events will enjoy the fate of the "skeleton."

The traditional skiing and skating events have stood the test of time. To demonstrate improvement (unfortunately, innovative equipment is more important than expertise), speed is still the principal objective.

The solution is to retain the traditional events and to eliminate the "half-pipe" approach to Olympic greatness. The winter Olympics should mirror the summer Olympics and concentrate on the physical development of homo sapiens including speed, endurance, size, and technique. The large bumps at the top of the mountain (moguls) sully the Olympic spirit.

○ ○ ○

In a *Wall Street Journal* article, a special report once itemized the foodstuffs consumed by the sixteen-member United States ski team for 1,255 meals for two weeks at the Nagano Winter Olympics in Japan. Assuming three meals per day, sixteen people would normally eat 672 meals; therefore, it is clear that the US skiers averaged more than five meals per day and/or the trainers, coaches, women skiers, and alumni were eligible for culinary paradise.

If that statistic is not shocking, would you believe that 500 pounds of carved meat (almost one pound per meal including breakfast), 400 pints of ice cream, 144 loaves of bread, and seventy cases of pizzas were consumed.

If those totals do not create concern, take a moment to evaluate the rationale. "The Alpine skiers were uptight about a diet of nuts and berries and sushi that would get pretty old (read boring) after a week." If the United States team had won several medals, the words of art might have been appropriate.

The Nagano story is fascinating. Why are not the sports pages of newspapers and magazines in the United States filled with tidbits about the lifestyle of our major athletes (other than drugs and booze)? It is true that American sources paid for the meals for the skiing team either through direct subsidy or contributions. The purpose of those payments is "news."

The press story should reflect the more important elements of culture. How many shot putters opt for single rooms? How do the divers react to the local art museum? What books do mogul skiers read? What are the favorite restaurants of the speed skaters? Where do hockey players purchase their clothes? How many luge participants attend the opera? Are there any Democrats in the group?

Did the majority of the athletes at Nagano eat in a comparable fashion to the skiers? If so, the swimmers might gain muscle tone and lose speed. Unless they break the law, we are seldom informed that our athletes are complex human beings. The *Wall Street Journal* has discharged a critical service.

○ ○ ○

When we consider the Olympics, we revere the virtues of amateurism and the joys of competition. Forget it!

The United States Olympic Committee, and its commercial supporters, have changed the character of the Olympics. The unadvertised, and seldom reported, bonuses for Olympic distinction have virtually eliminated the amateur designation. For example, in hockey, there is not any distinction between amateur and professional.

In past Olympics, the joy and challenge of competition, and a possible medal, were the exclusive rewards. By the year 2000, at Sydney, the rewards also became monetary.

Avery Brundage introduced a prize of $65,000 for every United States swimmer who won a gold medal. In soccer, every player on a gold medal team was entitled to $125,000. Even a gold medal winner in wind-surfing, not the most jingoistic sport, was entitled to $15,000. The same prize applied to a winner in kayak or canoe. Six hundred athletes from the United States participated in the Sydney Olympics.

For a gold medal in any event, a track participant was entitled to $15,000; each placing runner-up to $10,000, and for the bronze medal, $7,500 from the US Olympic Committee.

National governing bodies for each sport added to the USOC monetary totals. For example, in swimming, $50,000 was added for the gold medal. In soccer, a minimum of $2,000 per winning game was available for each player. To compound a felony, General Motors awarded new Cadillacs to synchronized swimmers who won gold medals and approved a $3.5 million program to purchase new automobiles for one hundred other US medal winners.

The only athletes who were ineligible for significant cash awards were the United States professional basketball players. Each player was to pay $150,000 for the privilege of qualifying for hundreds of thousands of dollars in endorsements. In addition, the gold medal check in basketball was made available to charity with the obvious impact of publicity.

A generation ago, Mark Spitz received seven gold medals in swimming (1972) without realizing a cash return from the USOC or US corporations. When he attempted to capitalize commercially, after he completed the Olympics, the public reaction was negative.

Recently, the United States was not the only guilty party. Russia awarded $100,000 to each gold medal recipient, Lithuania $400,000, Latvia $165,000, and Estonia was able to scrape up $65,000.

For the 2002 Winter Olympics, the United States increased the monetary track prize to $25,000 for the gold medal, an increase of $10,000 over Sydney; $15,000 for the silver and $7,500 for the bronze (the same as the previous Olympics).

The definition of "amateur" has been changed appreciably. With commercial additions, the USOC monetary prizes only reflect the tip of the iceberg. For the former communist countries, the amount of the prizes is more significant because the commercial benefits are limited.

If you are selected for the Olympics, be sure to determine the species of automobile which you would prefer.

○ ○ ○

The Peace Corps requires each volunteer to complete a pre-assignment training program, usually in the United States, which exposes the volunteer to the language and culture of the host country.

Based on overseas performance, it is pertinent to suggest that our summer and winter Olympic team members should be enrolled in a comparable orientation session. Obviously, the language of the host nation would be ignored in deference to demonstrated American limitations in foreign languages and the predominant need to discharge a more critical training requirement.

The young American athletes would be introduced to basic social customs. The curriculum would include using the novel words "please," "excuse me," and "thank you"; manifesting a semblance of humility; devising vocabulary to replace "ya know" and "yeah"; speaking basic English without chewing gum; pronouncing the name of the city where the Olympic Games will be staged; asking an occasional question; listening to the television interviewer's query before mumbling, "I owe it all to Mom"; learning the proper uses of the American flag, and recognizing that representing your country is an honor rather than a personal privilege.

Until they open their mouths, I am proud of America's Olympic representatives. When they speak, my patriotism is in jeopardy. Since media personalities have been programmed to ask five basic questions, our potential Olympic heroes and heroines could assimilate the complex answers before leaving American soil.

The beneficial impact of this essential training would not necessarily guarantee success in the "quest for gold," but we might make a few friends abroad. Of greater importance, our Olympians would be prepared for the inevitable next step in their career development: reading television commercials.

5

The Impact of Society on Sports

As a youngster, my heroes were sports figures (including the older boy who lived next door who was a high school athlete) and an occasional public service celebrity. The heroes of the current generation are scarce. When all roads lead to privatization, it is normal to cite an entrepreneur; however, most entrepreneurs with name recognition are "using" their stockholders and employees or operating at the edge of the law.

Sports figures are either paid exorbitant wages or are in disgrace. Between the two world wars, Babe Ruth was partially protected. The media was more concerned about his athletic ability than his extracurricular interests.

Without heroes, it is more difficult to aspire. In the glare of instantaneous global communications, it is unlikely that the least desirable human traits can be disguised while exploits in the arena are emphasized.

In spite of preoccupation with the indiscretions of athletes, they enjoy a semblance of esteem with the general public while heads of state, college presidents, and legislators are not revered. It is tempting to deal with the facts: the professional athlete makes a fortune, provides comic relief, and is seldom held accountable. Ignore that cynical comparison and step inside the stadium.

In athletics, the results are definitive. You win or you lose (except in ice hockey where tie games and extraordinary violence are the order of the day). The nuances are lost in translation. Even in individual sports, the result is controlling and transcends the expertise, and the societal behavior, of the players.

In contrast, the political or institutional leader is a walking nuance; a person saddled with an unresolved game called life, operating with minimal rules in a complex society. It is rather difficult to identify with a person of that ilk.

Currently, there are few heroes in athletics but not because of increased media scrutiny or the expansion of the leagues in several sports. The real culprit is advertising that has eliminated the "human factor" from celebrities of all kinds, and nurtured extravagant salaries and lifestyles, and television "talking heads." Cal Ripkin was an exception but he was loyal, competent, team oriented, and reasonable.

○ ○ ○

It is a disturbing that even the most accommodating friend can manifest deep concern about the outcome of a friendly tennis match. With alacrity, your opponent can change from a friend or compatible associate into a blustering, unsmiling villain in quest of victory.

In athletics, concentration is essential, and a desire to win is a prerequisite for success; however, winning must be placed in context, even at Wimbledon or Yankee Stadium. That context is reasonable interpersonal relationships both on and off the court or gridiron. In contemporary sports, an inordinate will to win can provoke a split personality, violence, abuse, or at the very least, discourtesy.

Why is it more enjoyable to lose to a superb player, in any individual sport, rather than to triumph, or lose, over one of your caliber? The superior player represents a challenge. Life fosters the hope of attainment rather than perpetuating the norm. If the goal is realistic, the quest is usually meaningless; therefore, only the result is vital. If the objective (competition per se) fails to stimulate, the requisite incentive is missing.

We should always look up to insure a winning perspective, but not too far. If we have a reasonable chance to win, remember the rules and the pleasure of participation. Winning is *not* everything.

$\bigcirc \ \bigcirc \ \bigcirc$

The skills required by a pitcher in baseball and a quarterback in football are unique in the victory-oriented athletic world. When compensation was related to skill, rather than the turnstile, pitchers and quarterbacks were rewarded with the highest salaries on a reasonable scale. Now, a home run from a player with a .231 batting average is considered the epitome of skill, and the inane jig of the tight-end after catching an easy touchdown pass is considered the ultimate grace.

The pitcher and the quarterback must hone native and acquired skills to a level of perfection seldom reached by athletes discharging relatively unskilled roles. It is a pity that admiring fans fail to recognize, or appreciate, the disparate, complex skills required to throw a quick-breaking curve with precision to the low, inside corner or to "thread the needle" with a short football pass up the middle. Of equal importance, the baseball pitcher and the football quarterback control the eventual outcome with the choice of pitch or play (increasingly sent from the sideline but still important with last-second changes).

The roar of the crowd bears little relationship to the skill factor. As usual, in contemporary society, skill takes a back seat to hubris, bravado, profit, and victory.

$\bigcirc \ \bigcirc \ \bigcirc$

Texas secondary school officials have decreed that high school athletes would not be allowed to participate in interscholastic sports unless they attained a passing grade in each academic subject. The edict caused a major flap. The state legislature and the governor took sides.

I would much prefer to give the student athlete permission to attend classes providing that he or she succeeds in athletics. If a student fails to make the grade as an outstanding athlete, he or she could continue to try to make the team, but access to the classroom would be denied unless a varsity letter were earned or the quest for athletic participation were discontinued.

You may think that this proposal is silly but consider the constructive results. Many of the superior athletes would not want to waste time attending classes. They would work in gas stations until their biceps were recognized by the collegiate and professional scouts. Since they would not possess high school diplomas, they would bypass the collegiate experience and proceed directly to the professional ranks. The best academic students would do their utmost on the playing field or shun athletics. High school sports would be placed in perspective.

The slogan in Texas was: "No pass—No play." Under my revised system, the slogan in football which is the only high school sport in which Texans are interested, would be: "Control Your Body to Develop Your Mind."

Under the approved system, imagine the plight of a bright quarterback in a music class who happens to have a tin ear. One failing grade, even in music, and he will be forced to leave the gridiron.

In Texas, is there not some incentive other than removal from the field of sports to induce teenagers to study? If athletically-prone Texas educators were replaced by a few folks with educational priorities, the quality of the secondary schools might be improved.

At the University of Maine, Work Study funds provided by the Federal Government were utilized to compensate students for watching the daily regimen of football players on a covert basis.

The University of Maine CIA contingent was paid with Federal tax dollars for trailing football players and reporting absences from class and other infamous crimes. The jocks were then confronted with the infractions. If the culprits did not reform, they lost the gift automobiles and free luxurious apartments presented by grateful alumni. I am exaggerating slightly, but at no point did the University of Maine suggest that academic performance was germane.

If a varsity football player, receiving Federal funds, attended class, the academic experience was complete. The scholarship remained in force. Attendance, I assume, produced the requisite "C" grade that insured continuing access to the shoulder pads. If the Federal Work Study funds were used to promote academic attainment, the enabling act would probably be declared unconstitutional.

○ ○ ○

Why do not more Black and Hispanic professional athletes donate a tithe of their salary for the support of inner-city schools?

In contemporary society, essential tax allocations at the federal and state levels are seldom authorized for remedial support for predominately Black, urban, public school systems. Private foundations lack the financial resources or the institutional will, and the affected parents are poor or preoccupied with survival.

Since baseball is the national pastime, and football is runner-up, and since young Blacks consider successful Black athletes role models, professional athletes could easily support the urban public school educational programs in major cities.

In the United States, salary level is related to choice of profession and luck (whether you manufacture mouthwash or play right field). Where salary level is deemed personal entitlement, carrying unique rights and privileges by those anointed to receive the financial blessing of a market-oriented society, a tithe for school support would be unusual. If a nation refuses to compensate outstanding teachers on a competitive basis, a voluntary charitable gesture with positive impact would be unlikely to materialize.

The current motto is "take it and run." For professional athletes, there is an additional fringe benefit. Accept your salary, strike, fail to "run," and continue to receive compensation from the union.

A modicum of equity in the salary structure must prevail. In the absence of pressure from the electorate, voluntary salary-balancing remedies will never "fly." On the other hand, if a few professional players took the initiative, professional athletes in all of the major sports would follow suit, and urban core teacher's salaries could be raised a notch.

Professional athletes receive astronomical salaries because fans pay huge prices for tickets. If college professors discharge their assignments with distinction (in fields such as business), there is a direct correlation between income-producing results for alumni and faculty salaries.

The same phenomenon applies to the salary structure for collegiate faculty involved with athletics. In higher education, salaries are only exemplary when the sport attracts fans in droves. Generally, professors and staff receive salaries which are unusually high only in fields where business or major sports are involved.

If I attend a sports event or enjoy a meal in a restaurant, the benefits are immediate and tangible. With most college degrees, time intervenes, and the graduate is convinced that compensation is related to his or her innate abilities rather than to a relevant education.

The salaries of teachers and athletes reflect the basic values of society. We would rather be entertained at the moment than to acknowledge that distinguished teaching has been a prime factor. The educator will always be suspect since he or she is involved with the world of ideas that are difficult to relate to the marketplace. An average person may make a fortune or throw a football; however, teachers are essential and they should be compensated adequately in every field. Teachers must receive competitive compensation or society will suffer.

○ ○ ○

A university is not the natural situs for competitive team sports. It would be less costly, and more effective, for the athletes and the academics, to allow cities and communities, rather than colleges and universities, to sponsor amateur athletic teams. If they were interested and qualified, college students would be able to affiliate with the teams located within reasonable proximity to the campus. No academic credit would be given for such participation. If the college student excelled as an athlete, he or she would be eligible to proceed to the next level as a professional athlete. Intercollegiate athletics would be removed from the college equation.

For a short period of time, the alumni would be unhappy; however, as the municipal amateur teams evolved, the college alumni would support the community teams. Professional teams would also be interested in lending financial support to their community "feeder" system. Universities could then return to basic academic pursuits. Higher education would once again stress academic attainment.

I realize that my proposal is impractical, but consider the superb teams that would be developed in major cities where a dozen colleges were located. The quality of athletic performance would be commendable. Outstanding athletes, from all sources, would have a meaningful choice. Most college students would graduate, and college financial resources would be applied to the quality of education.

○ ○ ○

When do you recognize that you are losing your physical facility? Unless you slam your finger in a car door (I have suffered that experience), the loss of physical dexterity or stamina appears to be gradual and unnoticed. For a half century, I engaged in organized exercise/sports by design. Until the last decade, when I emerged as a social security recipient, my speed, expertise, and stamina have been gradually diminished. Is physical conditioning really a deterrent (partial) to the aging process?

When I was a relative youngster, I preached that age was a frame of mind rather than a physical reality. Today, I am aware of the truth.

For approximately one-half century, a person, if he or she has been generally healthy, is prepared to cope physically. At least psychologically, he or she should be prepared to cope. In an emergency, he or she feels that it would be possible to run the first or the last mile, climb the ladder, lift the weight, stand the vigil, or negotiate the hurdle. If threat is a factor, it is anticipated that the threat will be met directly.

If physical restraint is necessary, for domestic peace and tranquility, the requisite dose will be applied. Even though practical application is unnecessary, the spirit of Walter Mitty is in operation (once again).

As mentioned previously, for the first 50 years (excluding pre-puberty), in the presence of overt physical strength, there is only limited discomfort. On the contrary, there is a bit of pride in contemplation of physical self-awareness and a sense of well-being stimulated by perceived physical facility.

On the day that a person becomes 50, physical security is replaced by doubt. The younger males appear larger, louder, ruder, and potentially more violent. Physical surroundings may appear intimidating. Traffic, controlled by younger males, becomes personally threatening. Physical conditioning becomes a secondary goal.

At age 40, a person may not be able to run as fast or as far as at 20, but he or she either thinks that it is possible or does not think about it at all. At age 50, physical deterioration is self-evident. No combination of diet, exercise, sexual activity, or positive thought will alter that reality. The aches and pains of exercise create the aches and pains of living with age. Exercise becomes therapy rather than a chapter in the joy of living.

At 50, give or take a few birthdays, even if you are healthy and fit, the physical dimension becomes more important and less amenable to control. Each growth is potentially cancer, rather than a blemish to the ego, and each pain is probably arthritis rather than a reflection of physical activity.

When you are younger, a larger man appears merely larger. At 50, an approaching giant becomes formidable. As we are prepared to accomplish less physically, physical challenges become ominous rather than part of daily life. When taking a short walk, the distance seems to expand, and the role as spectator becomes more acceptable.

I am convinced that some people treat age as a crutch and succumb to premature physical senility. I also realize that each succeeding year makes me less able to cope with the physical dimension. Now that I am "over the hill," the issue is moot.

O O O

I do not understand women's attraction to men. Supposedly, they do not notice a man's physique. If the bloke is kind, with an eighty-eight pound frame, the women "go ape" (pardon the male jingoism).

Baloney! When women suggest that they do not care about "buns," or biceps, they are either protecting a fragile marriage, addicted to an alternate sexual preference, or afraid to be honest.

It all depends upon what a woman, married, single or whatever, enjoys ogling. In self-defense, she may claim that "bald is beautiful." When her bald, vegetating husband is "on the road," that same woman will purchase a body-building magazine, enjoy male burlesque, watch a football locker room interview, or bake cookies.

When Maria Shriver married "Conan the Terrible," there was a bit of envy in the typical feminist reaction. It is not pure accident that physical attraction is important between the sexes.

For a male, a good physique is a decided asset (as it is for a woman). Even men who prefer men do not object to bulging biceps. A kind word will carry the day, but a solid physique will start the day on the right foot. If you are under 50, physical appearance, even on the masculine side of the equation, sells magazines.

Media Reactions

Sports figures represent a mirror image of American society. When an athletic hero acts like a child, sportswriters have a field day.

If John McEnroe had a temper tantrum in the middle of a match or Roger Clemens hurled splintered bats as well as baseballs at Yankee Stadium, the sports pages were inundated with juvenile commentary. If McEnroe wrote a poem, or Clemens utilized two six-letter words in the same paragraph, the sports writers would be out to lunch.

When Wade Boggs discarded his Yankee uniform in cities where away games were played, and was frequently observed with the same mistress in tow, sports writers were titillated by this human behavior.

If a professional athlete were to write a comparative article about the cultural attributes of urban centers on the circuit, the results might be edifying. On the other hand, if it pays to be childlike, what is the incentive?

A generation ago, a Federal judge, in a moment of profundity, decreed that women sportswriters cannot be denied access to male locker rooms. That enlightened ruling is being challenged periodically in a variety of cases which are being tried in the daily newspapers. The coaches and players who protest are being censured for their refusal to allow women reporters access to men's locker rooms to view seminude sports figures behaving as the emotional children they are.

It is alleged that women's place is everywhere; however, we still maintain separate toilet facilities. Although this condition may also pass, it is still appropriate for men (predominantly) to be killed in the front lines of the contemporary version of war.

Even if we utilize gender-less restroom facilities, I am convinced that women should be excluded from men's athletic locker rooms (and vice versa) not because the temporary inhabitants are seminude, but because media coverage should not be discharged in a team locker room or in the bathroom of a private home.

Following an athletic event, the players should be provided with a few private moments in which to shower, to dress for the outside world, and to replace the grim intensity of the playing forum with a more sedate format. We do not ask the negotiating teams at a peace conference to meet the press in the shower room, and the circumstances are comparable.

The owners of professional sports teams are affluent. They could easily provide a press lounge where sports reporters of variable gender proclivities could meet the players informally. The players would be relatively composed (my weakest argument) and would be less likely to emulate immature men and women who have devoted many of their formative years to perfecting a game. The sports writers would be able to conduct normal interviews. The resulting articles might deal with the nuances of the game rather than with the immature trappings of the athletes.

The athletic locker room is not the athlete's castle, or the last bastion of male or female domination, or even a remnant of affirmative action. It is a refuge where the athletes prepare to return to the real world. In a separate media room, provided by team management which pays virtually nothing for public relations, and receives major coverage free, athletes and sportswriters of all persuasions could practice their essential roles.

The Federal case should be overruled. The locker room is misplaced on the sports page.

○ ○ ○

Until I was slightly mature, I watched a few college football bowl games on television. I endured several in succession, from Sugar to Rose, and exhausting hours later, I was hard-pressed to distinguish a Cornhusker from a Trojan.

The therapy was essential, but I did not enjoy the ambience, the results, or the endless blather. An occasional play generated remembrance of times past; however, those few moments were inundated with repetitive, inane commercials and a stream of meaningless comments from a legion of bogus experts and neophytes.

Infrequently, a former coach who knew the game of football would rise beyond the challenge of Basic English and impart useful information. Former players with limited education, an occasional college degree, no coaching experience, and inordinate hubris, monopolized the limitless time available for commentary.

In January 1999, I spent one Sunday afternoon watching sports on television. First, the remarkable New York Jets professional football team, under the tutelage of guru Bill Parcells, defeated Jacksonville to advance within a single rung of the Super Bowl.

The football game was followed by the number one ranked University of Connecticut women's basketball team playing the number two ranked University of Tennessee. Unfortunately, from the perspective of a former president, UCONN lost to a superior team.

The reason that I am devoting space to sports on television is related to the negative impact of subhuman commercials on the joy of watching tussles in which I have more than a passing interest. (Pay-as-you-go could not generate the essential gross income.)

In past years, asinine commercials were confined to timeouts, injuries, the ends of quarters, and half-time. Even in basketball, there were several offensive, but reasonable, breaks for the irrelevance of advertising.

Now, in professional football, commercials are actually featured between plays. If the present trend continues, there will be a commercial break while the football is in the air.

I mute the television set during the commercials and attempt to read. The continuity of the game is destroyed, and it is pure luck to rejoin the game at the proper moment.

In the 2002 Super Bowl football game staged in New Orleans, the New England Patriots defeated the heavily-favored St. Louis Rams on a forty-seven yard field goal with only a few seconds remaining.

Bill Bilichick, the former defensive coordinator for Bill Parcells and the New York Jets, is now the New England head coach. In the St. Louis game, he did a masterful job of preparation and game execution. From the opening kickoff, he was several strides ahead of the more talented Rams team. The smarter team, not the better team, won. For the first time since 1986, the Patriots appeared in the Super Bowl. For the first time in an eon, the City of Boston honored the national champion in a major sport. Not since the "hail Mary" last minute touchdown pass in a Boston College bowl game has a Boston team of any flavor won a championship. The athletic supporters, or maybe the denizens who admire the winner in any pursuit, overflowed when the Patriots returned to Boston.

Fox television carried the game. The commentators were outstanding, but, as usual, the commercials were gauche and disturbing. A generation ago, professional sports were provided with equal time. Now, the vapid, meaningless commercials, representing bad taste and marginal products, are predominate. The language is atrocious. The actors are failing to act, and relevant content has disappeared. If more than ten commercials were presented sequentially, I left the room and did the dishes.

The persons who enjoy watching sports on television have learned to ignore the commercials rather than expressing concern. Since the voting public (in 2004) disregards the content of Dubya's speeches, the reaction is not surprising. The electronic age has been extremely effective in creating hype rather than substance.

The commercials which constitute the major offenders are increasingly devoid of humor or content. The culture which they depict is the antithesis of the culture I enjoy.

O O O

Jack Sharkey is dead. As a sports devotee, I accept boxing as one of the genre with reluctance, but when a "world" champion dies in any sport, readers are attracted.

In concocting the pathos to justify a Pulitzer nomination, the sports writer referred to Mr. Sharkey as "colorful" which in this case is a euphemism for "depraved."

It is true that a colorful personality may reflect spirited or striking traits, but the word is being used with a lack or precision when a lifetime of cheating, debauchery, and dirty tricks is being depicted. Richard Nixon was not colorful merely because he made headlines. Jack Sharkey was not colorful merely because he was out of control. I prefer character to color in sports and in politics. A controlled person can reflect a vivid or colorful personality, but I suppose that only aberrational behavior sells newspapers.

O O O

As all sports fans are aware, Micky Mantle had his liver replaced. The fact that he was an alcoholic, and was suffering from lung cancer, did not limit his instantaneous access to a donated organ for which the waiting list was significant.

At a press conference following the transplant, Mr. Mantle stated, "Everything I have is wore out." In a subsequent story which appeared in *The New York Times*, sports writer Allen Myerson amended the quote to "worn out."

If a sports writer wants to punish an athlete, the illiterate language appears as stated. If hero worship is a factor, the language is revised to meet minimal standards.

If the actual quotation is incorporated, the language is grating and offensive. If the language is improved, a false impression of the athlete is conveyed. In my opinion, the actual language is germane. Young, impressionable readers of the sport pages should be aware that attainment on the playing field or in the classroom is equally important.

○ ○ ○

In May 2000, prior to her first doubles match in the French Open, which marked her return to professional tennis after several years of retirement, Martina Navratilova, at age 43, held a press conference.

A few of her comments were edifying. She referred to the Agassi-Graf romance as "a very unlikely couple. They seem to have a great time together. Steffi is like a groupie now." In commenting on younger players, Ms. Navratilova stated: "I would still like to help some youngster." In evaluating Martina Hingis she said: "She would be hard to beat. It will be interesting to see how the public responds to her after last year. I thought they were a little hard on her."

In featuring this uninformative, basic interview without substance, the Associated Press disclosed that Navratilova "is still the champion of the candid comment, speaking her mind with a wit and wisdom beyond other players."

I am unaware of the manifestations of wit and wisdom to which the Associated Press reporter has been exposed, but his or her familiarity with erudition and satire has been severely limited. I agree that Navratilova occasionally employs a word with five letters, but even Yogi Berra emulated that standard, and he was (unintentionally) witty.

○ ○ ○

Ten years ago, the word "arguably" existed (it was coined in 1610), but it was relegated to the monasteries edition of the unabridged dictionary. Today, arguably, it appears at least once on every sports page.

What does "arguably" mean? It should make reference to a statement or opinion which is subject to actual dispute, but when the typical sportswriter heads the word toward the goal post, it is intended to refer to distinction limited by unanticipated objection. For example, "Roger Clemens, arguably the best pitcher in the American League . . ."

Why get exercised about the frequent, and possibly erroneous, use of a word? When I was a lad, "it's him" was a perversion. Today, if you say "it's he," you are perverted. That is not problematic or even arguable.

Speaking of Roger Clemens, *The New York Times* lead on the first sports page stated that the "Yankees Clemens Appears to Have an Extension in Hand." I assumed that he was suffering the advanced stages of Dupuytren's Contracture. In fact, the "extension" potential referred to the status of contractual negotiations.

Headline writers for the sports section suffer the same deficiencies as other hired "hands."

In the 1948 movie, *Apartment for Peggy*, Jeanne Craine manifested the ability to use statistics without the requisite factual basis.

To illustrate the "without a fact in sight" syndrome, I have been informed by an unimpeachable source that 87 percent of the people who read the sports pages never participated in sports. Obviously, the typical "letter to the editor" originates with one of those incorporated in the 87 percent.

Invariably at a social function, not related to athletics, somebody will make a sports reference to a statistic, an injury, a character, or a social defect. As the mesmerizing conversation unfolds, it is clear that the speaker is not wearing, or never wore, an athletic supporter. For the distaff side, we should probably use "jumper" in both contexts.

I am not deprecating the practice. You do not have to be deceased to read an obituary. On the other hand, if you have been a participant in sports, you seldom have an identity crisis when you read about the prima donnas, entrepreneurs, and convicts who inhabit the sports world. When I participated in sports, there was more than a casual reference to the "team" or to the "spirit" of the occasion. Sport teams now appear to be only a platform for the many athletes who become affluent.

Back to the point! Whenever I meet a person who is interested in sports, there is a momentary thrill of possible shared experience until he or she resorts to bogus statistics.

○ ○ ○

A decade ago, my favorite team sport may have absorbed a mortal blow. For the first time in history, the unrequited greed of owners and players motivated the cancellation of the remainder of the professional baseball schedule including the World Series. Baseball has become a business. The only solution, which will not occur, is to apply the Federal Antitrust laws to a former sport.

Without describing the sordid details, I would like to submit a constructive proposal. Sports writers and commentators must honor a walkout strike pertaining to baseball exclusively. For the indefinite future, not one word about major league baseball will be printed or aired. A few diehard fans may attend an occasional game, but in the absence of daily statistics, depiction of player moral lapses, and endless analysis of physical injuries, interest in the alleged "game" would disappear. If the players were judged by athletic skill rather than acting ability on and off the field, it might become enjoyable to identify with the national pastime. If any baseball reporter violates the ban, he or she will be forced to attend all future negotiating sessions involving owners and the players' union.

Within one week of the imposition of this publication edict, settlement of the strike would occur miraculously. Without publicity, baseball would revert to its original status as a game.

The price of a ticket is related to hype. If hype were eliminated, the price of a ticket would drop significantly. Publicity about baseball is the lifeblood of a lucrative business. If those who produce the hype refused to follow the "game plan," baseball owners and players would find a rationale for negotiation.

Because my solution will dictate a settlement, we will never return to the halcyon days when baseball was merely a sport. On the other hand, for one week it would be pure joy to read the sports pages without the soap opera which has evolved from the reporting of a remarkable game. For a short time, let's ask the media to play "hard ball."

Discrimination

In 1996, the Acting Commissioner of Baseball, who happened to be an owner, imposed a one-year suspension on Ms. Margie Schott, the managing partner of the Cincinnati Reds. During that period, Ms. Schott was not allowed to direct the fortunes of the Reds. Her stock portfolio remained intact. As a person with average education and experience, what was the nature of her crime?

In a television interview, she stated that Adolf Hitler "was good in the beginning, but that he just went too far." The context of her statement was not provided in any media report.

The statement, on the face of it, does not reflect prejudice. Hitler, in the first few years, did, as Ms. Schott alleged, "build tremendous highways and get all the factories going." If she had only added that he subsequently created the Holocaust, the television interview would probably have been ignored. Ms. Schott apologized for her statement, but that act merely fueled the fire.

In 1992 and 1993, Ms. Schott made ethnic and racial slurs. She was suspended for the 1993 baseball season and fined $25,000. The adverse reaction to her most recent statement was evaluated in the context of previous statements. Her punishment was based on an accumulation of sins.

The Commissioner of Baseball stated that, "We in no way concur with her interpretation of history." The assistant director of the Anti-Defamation League decreed that Ms. Schott needed "training regarding the meaning of the word 'prejudice' and on the Holocaust." The assistant director further stated that if she had mentioned "the Jews and the Holocaust that would have been nice." The context of Ms. Schott's comments re progress in Germany in the early thirties was not reported.

I am confident that Ms. Schott's comments about Blacks, Jews, and Hitler's Germany, based on several interviews, were offensive. Undoubtedly, she is a suspect character, but she should have been evaluated based on the actual quotations, at a specific time, rather than an accumulation of imprecise statements which did not provide a context. Consolidating her comments over a period of years without any background information is unfair.

The Commissioner of Baseball and the assistant director of the Anti-Defamation League need "a bit of training concerning prejudice and the Holocaust." Hitler was a menace. The Holocaust was an abomination. For a limited period of time, at the beginning of his reign, he sponsored essential reforms which pleased the German people. If Ms. Schott intended to make the distinction between progress and subsequent illegal and immoral acts, she may have been in error not to provide the comparison. At the same time, the Commissioner and the acting director made mistakes.

Ms. Schott needed to return to school (elementary), but the other characters in the plot did not qualify as her teachers.

If I alleged that Black men do not become distinguished Certified Public Accountants, I would be accused of racism. When a 1992 movie was released, entitled: *White Men Can't Jump*, it was considered humorous rather than racist. Ignore the pole vault, the high jump, dressage, the steeplechase, and the javelin, events in which Whites are predominate but not necessarily "better." The movie concentrates on basketball.

Even in basketball, there are a handful of Whites who can get both feet off the floor at the same time, but let us agree that Blacks generally out-jump Whites.

If that statement is true, any comparative racial references should be fair game. "Blacks are inferior at fly fishing." "Hispanics are inferior at ski jumping." The obvious answer is that exposure and training are controlling. It would require extensive scientific research before genes could be cited. Blacks in the USA inner cities concentrate on basketball as youngsters in Latin America concentrate on baseball and soccer.

It is undoubtedly true that Blacks excel at jumping in basketball. As the result of racial sensitivity and research in the United States, there are few sports reported where Whites appear to excel. It would not be acceptable to suggest that many Whites have been excellent as baseball pitchers, as football quarterbacks, or as computer inventors.

When you prepare a balance sheet, jumping high is normally an asset unless you are a partner in an accounting firm or the basketball net is raised two feet. If this analysis is pursued, I will lose the reader's goodwill. That would be a liability for a person of any hue.

○ ○ ○

Sally is 40 years of age and a paraplegic. Two years ago, she was severely injured in an automobile accident. Her spinal cord was damaged with permanent loss of movement in both legs.

Sally was a marathon runner and an outstanding tennis player. The physical therapy following the accident was helpful. Her general attitude was positive, but she gave the impression that she had "given up." The medical profession does not express any hope for improvement. Her friends suggest that a "miracle" is possible, but Sally would like to continue her life through a limited physical perspective. She is continuing her avocational interest in painting, and her family has become her major commitment.

Being in a wheelchair permanently is a horrible result of the luck of the die. Against formidable odds, Sally is now leading a "normal" life.

Based on the stereotype of courage, Sally is expected to believe that she "will run another marathon." In real life, Sally represents the truth associated with a severe handicap. She has already performed a miracle. To expect her to aspire to return to her original priorities creates a meaningless objective in her mind that is the antithesis of her perceived expectation.

○ ○ ○

In the media coverage of sports, there is a preoccupation with injury. The incidence of injury in all levels of the athletic hierarchy is exceptionally high. It is understandable that injuries can be a logical result of repeated participation in competitive sports.

On the other hand, for many sports reporters a preoccupation has become an obsession. Sports press conferences seem to rely upon injuries as the leitmotif. Athletes learn to discuss even minor injuries in elaborate detail. The responses are seldom related to significant facts but tend to stress the superficial and the mundane.

The media infatuation with injury does not normally incorporate a treatment regimen, a precise medical analysis, or an emphasis on facts. The subjective reactions of the athlete are featured. Rather than recognizing the importance of precision, the portrayal of sports injury reflects a minimal, distorted view of the condition rather than a commitment to medical reality.

If the sports writers were to deal intelligently with the substance of athletic injuries, the reading public would be informed. Of greater importance, the officials in sports who review the basic rules might take steps to restrict the danger of injury. For example, in the last half century of football games, the injuries have increased geometrically, but the equipment worn and the precautions taken by the players have not been altered appreciably. If the reading public were educated concerning injuries, the pressure to alter playing rules might become significant.

If all other remedies fail, it might be preferable to report that "a broken left leg will require five weeks for recovery. Period."

○ ○ ○

In college, there are several "lightweight" athletic categories. In football and crew, there are weight limitations. In boxing and wrestling, there are weight classes. With freshmen teams, even the year in college is a factor. With the exception of weight scales and height bars in medical offices and height limitations for the US Air Force Academy aviator program, we do not usually restrict height and weight in American society. A coxswain in crew is usually light, by choice, but only one seat on a commercial aircraft is allocated to a three-hundred-pound passenger. A seat at the cinema accommodates viewers of all sizes. As basketball players become taller, they will be able to "dunk" from a sitting position. It would appear that unless you are committed to killing the other guy in boxing, wrestling, or war, the sky is generally the limit regarding height and weight requirements.

The time has come to recognize that we are breeding monsters who can use their bulk to play professional sports. In professional football, defensive linemen now exceed three hundred pounds. A generation ago, two hundred and fifty pounds was gigantic. As the result of increased size on the line, quarterbacks and running backs are more vulnerable and few escape the ignominy (or pain) of being sat upon by a truck or tackled at the knees by a derrick. Football runners are subjected to "pile ons," and they are then restricted to watching the games on television.

In professional basketball, shooting skill has little meaning unless the defense fails to guard the three-point shooter. The rebounding game now resembles water polo with only the seven footers above water.

Exceptionally tall and heavy athletes should compete with their own genre or the basic rules should be changed. A three- hundred-pound quarterback may not be able to leave the pocket with impunity, but he should be able to sit on one of those offensive, defensive linemen.

In 1988, the Dartmouth College students were up in arms (bows and arrows) because the name "Indians" to identify their intercollegiate athletic teams was perceived as discriminatory. For a century and a half, the Dartmouth "Indians" represented the college on the athletic fields of battle. The same issue was raised in Atlanta with the baseball "Braves" and in Washington, D.C., with the football "Redskins." Increasingly, such appellations are considered repugnant to native-born Americans.

Whether you are Red, White, or Black, history is being revamped to glorify the present and to eliminate past realities. This commitment will also disappear but not before subjectivity has run its course.

When I was a lad visiting Canada, we never referred to Canadians as "Canucks." Today, the professional Vancouver hockey team proudly displays that name. When I was a lad, "Blacks" were "Negroes," and you were guilty of gross discrimination to hint that "Blacks" were black. Clearly, the Washington Redskins must become the "Potomacs" (referring to the river not the Indian tribe), and the Atlanta Braves will become the "Cotton Pickers" when Whites pick the crop.

I was offended by the Hartford Whalers nickname, but I have always had an inordinate interest in fauna. The Cincinnati "Reds" jarred my political sensitivities and the San Diego "Padres" focused my concern about the separation of church and state. I was also indignant about nicknames for other sports teams when they confronted the ecology (e.g., the "Cardinals" and the "Hornets").

By what right do a bunch of adults who play children's games, under the banner of the Bruins, Tigers, Lions, and Cubs, continue with impunity? The Cardinals are seen in St. Louis even if they do not represent the church. When Blue Jays fly over Toronto, they may take umbrage. Who will defend our feathered and hirsute friends? Possibly, the Miami Heat or the Indiana Pacers will come to the rescue of the Penguins (Pittsburgh).

I have always been offended by the "Big Red" designation at Cornell University. Since my student days, I have assumed that the name refers to the color, not that a majority of Ithaca students, in contrast to their Hanover competitors, were raised on the reservation.

Before this complex issue is resolved, we should refer to Harvard teams as the "Cantabs" (not Crimson) to avoid embarrassment and assume that the Dartmouth students do not represent the subcontinent in Southeast Asia.

◯ ◯ ◯

In sports, "rights" are being exercised without corresponding restraint, much less responsibility. A few examples should suffice.

In Japan, professional baseball players are not allowed to dispute the decision of an umpire, but it is not suggested that the "rights" of the players are being curtailed. In contrast, we allow basketball coaches to attack students and to intimidate referees. We allow basketball players to commit mayhem without retribution (or only minimal punishment) including the choking of a coach. We allow hockey players to decapitate, figuratively, the opposition with the penalty confined to only two minutes of solitude (for most Americans a fate worse than death). The expulsion of unruly, and even violent fans and students, in virtually every "popular" sport, is rare. In many sports, we allow the fans to control the action, and occasionally the result.

In most demonstrations against duly constituted authority, freedom of expression (or the price of a ticket) rather than exercises in anarchy are considered the rationale. Meaningless, overt, combative, physical violence or verbal abuse, which is perpetrated for the television camera, is seldom followed by punitive action. Violence, physical and verbal, rather than the increasingly suspect ballot box, are becoming the focal points of freedom.

An episode from professional baseball is typical. In spring training, Rube Rivera, a potentially outstanding player for the New York Yankees, pilfered a bat and glove from star Derek Jeter's locker. He sold the loot for $2,500. After Mr. Rivera's crime was authenticated, his contract was voided. Authorities said that Mr. Rivera, who had participated in professional baseball for many years, had committed a "rookie's error." In past years, Dwight Gooden and Darryl Strawberry, among others, were also guilty of comparable "rookie errors" (including drugs, drunken driving, and other misdemeanors). Mike Tyson, the pugilist former heavyweight champion, enjoyed chomping the ear of a living opponent in the ring.

As usual with these indiscretions, Mr. Rivera was not subject to punitive action. He returned the stash to Mr. Jeter's locker, left the Yankees, and may play for another major league team. Now that Paula Jones and ice skater Tonya Harding have enjoyed a professional boxing encounter, Mike Tyson may have a worthy opponent.

The New York Times carried a statistical chart that depicted flagrant professional basketball fouls. If the current trend continues, the total will exceed the highest previous year by more than 20 percent. One of the New Jersey Nets committed his sixth flagrant foul of the season. The player involved will have missed a few games and was assessed approximately $350,000 in fines and salary. With millions in salary available, the fines are marginal.

Increasingly, over-aggressive play (a euphemism) in the National Basketball League is involving "the stars" who might be suspended for a few games. Basketball and hockey are not the only major sports that are experiencing increased player violence. The changing mores of society are having a direct negative impact on all collegiate and professional sports.

In a democracy, respect for institutions, and those responsible for them, is a sine qua non for an atmosphere in which freedom can be enjoyed. When those representing authority are attacked, ignored, deprecated with impunity, and paid considerably less than the participants for whom they are responsible, democracy is in jeopardy as well as in retreat.

The War on Drugs

Given the excessive salaries, sky-rocketing fringe benefits, commercial endorsements, and monetary awards available to successful athletes in a growing number of sports, it is naive to assume that pinpointed educational programs will reduce the use of drugs.

In recent history, a few nations have attempted to provide drugs for athletes participating in international competitions. The most notorious offender was East Germany during the score of years from 1970 to 1988. During that period, East Germany's triumphs in the men's and women's Olympics were extraordinary. Men and women were awarded a remarkable number of medals in track and field, swimming and speed skating. When the "Iron Curtain" was eliminated in 1989 with the cessation of one-party rule in East Germany, that country discontinued its proven use of drugs for athletes. Very few countries, with only marginal success, have attempted to control drug use among athletes through governmental decree.

In the United States, efforts to reduce or control drug abuse by athletes has been confined to private organizations. The controls have been administered by organizations charged with overseeing team sports. Until the last few years, the major thrust has been to control the sources of drugs rather than the recipients. When clocked times, and precise records, do not differentiate winners from losers, control efforts have been minimal. As a result, most of the testing has accentuated track and swimming. In addition, professional football and baseball players are being subjected to limited testing.

The 2003 efforts of major league baseball which traditionally refused to face the evil realities of drug abuse are edifying. A few years ago, major league professional baseball players, Jose Canesco and Ken Caminite, informed the media, on a voluntary basis, that they had utilized steroids in compiling impressive career home run records. They also alleged that more than half of the major league baseball players engaged in the practice.

As a result of these disclosures, the owners and players agreed reluctantly to random testing for the 2003 baseball season. If more than 5 percent of the players tested positively, minimal fines were to be levied.

In spite of advance notice, more than 5 percent of the players did not curtail the use of steroids. The immediate fines were ludicrous. Initial negative results would not include fines. When five indiscretions were detected, the user would be forced to absorb a $100,000 penalty or a single year suspension. International executives who control the use of drugs in sports labeled the baseball penalties projected in the United States "a complete joke."

Major league baseball officials did not consider that the results of steroidal use were offensive. Only a few who considered the impact on the long-term health of the violators raised objections to the minimal punishment assessed.

Organized baseball alleges that the players' use of THG designer steroids (tetrahydrogestrinome) is comparable to the fact that hundreds of thousands of American males use Viagra, and other steroids, to improve their lifestyle. This analogy is also ridiculous. National records are not being publicly certified pertaining to the individual use of Viagra.

Drug testing for athletes will never meet the challenge. Drug manufacturers will always win the race with those companies that market testing equipment. Drug substance users are anticipating every new testing device. Initially, those testing procedures were juvenile but effective (e.g., diet soda, eye drops, and urine-tampering gimmicks).

Currently, a Federal Grand Jury is investigating dietary supplements manufactured by Bay Area Laboratory Cooperative (Balco). Scores of professional athletes from football and baseball have been subpoenaed; however, it is likely that anti- testing devices will be concocted before meaningful statistics can be released. Initially, four National Football League players representing the Oakland Raiders have been cited.

The potential long-term physical impact of steroids is critical (heart disease, liver tumors). Steroids may limit the life of the user by ten years; however, the typical star player may assume the risk. Major sports records, where records are a significant factor, will reflect the efforts of long-ball hitters in baseball (for example) who accept the tradeoff for celebrity status and coveted wealth. If 90 percent of the long-ball hitters join the steroids parade, the 10 percent who opt to increase longevity will secure premature post-baseball employment or create a separate league to enjoy the sport of baseball. A home run is only a limited esthetic attainment.

In contrast to most other countries, the United States is making a concerted effort to monitor drug violations for the 2004 Athens Summer Olympics. The temptations for the world-class athlete to engage in drug use can become paramount. Until the coaches are able to control excessive abuse, most Olympic behavioral infractions will emphasize the innovative reliance upon drugs. A recent national opinion poll suggests that the use of steroids in the Olympics presents a more egregious problem than in the continental United States. Jingoism is a major factor when the United States is compared to other nations.

The prognosis regarding athletic drug abuse is not salutary. Human growth hormones have not yet been confronted with screening tests, and the fans are now searching for entertainment rather than performance. The cost of cleanup for all facets of drug abuse are prohibitive. Drug laboratories will continue to devise testing deterrents, and innocent athletes will discover that their innocence is also difficult to prove.

6

Pseudo-Sports

If hunting duck hunters were legal, the limit should be ignored.

In the United States, the number of hunters is still greater than the number of bird watchers. Although, more than one-half million conservationists (most of whom are bird watchers) have joined the National Audubon Society, several times that number blind ducks from duck blinds.

Given the constitutional anachronism enshrining the "right to bear arms," and the gross single-mindedness of the National Rifle Association, it is improbable that hunters will switch to canasta. The only option is to convert the hunter, with self-interest as the motivation, into a person with an eye for the ambience in which he or she hunts.

The prescription is simple. The cure (education) is elusive. Current educational programs should convince the hunter that preserving the hunting habitat is the only plan that will insure that his grandsons will have wild animals and game birds to exterminate. Controlled hunting is desirable. The transgressor, as with many issues in life, is abuse, rather than use.

Conservation must originate at the local level. Experience dictates that the sustained endeavors of a variety of interest groups are essential. Unfortunately, goodwill at the local level will not suffice.

Belatedly, we have also concluded that duck hunters must be concerned about the number of trout, the trees in the forest, and electing representatives who care.

The obstacles are formidable. In *Sports Afield*, hunting is considered a sport. The editor concluded: "To me, water always looks better when there is a fishing rod in the picture." He only found room in the issue for a short article entitled: "Nature," which recited the obvious distinctions between summer and fall.

We are what we read as well as what we eat. The writers of hunting and fishing propaganda must be committed to environmental realities before their readers will be able to claim that distinction.

The following suggestions may lead to a partial remedy: include conservation rather than prayer in the school curriculum; launch a clearinghouse which discharges a coordinating function for conservation groups; create a "Better Conservation Bureau" to police the environmental hucksters; and write a few letters to market-oriented, self-serving editors of "sporting" magazines requesting less bang for the "buck."

The earth may be destroyed by human aggression; however, banning the bomb may prove to be only a flimsy band-aid unless we save the environment for selected species of the duck and the darter, as well as for baby seals.

Do your utmost—write a letter to the editor of your favorite hunting or fishing journal.

Hunters represent an insensitive segment of American society. Since game wardens are in short supply (I have never met one), the hunters know that bag restrictions will not be observed. Few duck hunters have been exposed to a bird book. Water birds are difficult to identify, particularly ducks while flying. When a few ducks take off from the water, the hunter's reaction is instantaneous. With binoculars, distinguishing wing coloration is an art form. For most hunters, differentiating a Mallard from an endangered duck species presents a major challenge. Protected species meet the same fate as species which are subject to culling.

Assuming that noise, bag limits, and detection considerations are ignored, and duck hunters continue to enjoy the licensed privilege of killing designated duck species in season, on-the-scene enforcement is then essential.

If hunting is allowed as a sport, in order to compensate for the spoils, license fees should be increased significantly. In addition, the culling should be efficiently and relentlessly managed by the staff of the wildlife service in each state and by volunteer hunters commissioned to assist. Through indoctrination, culled species detection could be improved, and the spoils could be sold to commercial outlets. Overpopulation would be controlled, endangered species would be encouraged, the State treasury would be augmented to facilitate greater support for conservation, and the populace might be exposed to the exotic taste of wild duck.

If hunters who are hooked on gaming violations do not reform, the sentence must resort to an alternate athletic endeavor—lawn care. The euphoria associated with yard work is only excelled by eating, reading, sex, or participating in a team sport. If these options do not appeal to the hunting culprit, lawn care might constitute a viable alternative.

When I have completed the lawn chores, there is a unique form of relaxation that differs from the fatigue associated with athletics. The aerobics are equally constructive, but lawn and garden care include a generous dose of self-satisfaction. When you prune a tree, you are responding to nature's needs, improving your property, ignoring external reality, and maintaining your physical flexibility. To engage in clipping and pruning for an extensive period, requires a strong back and a weak mind. It also requires discipline.

The world will never recognize the tender loving care which I have bestowed on a number of lawns and gardens. As with most things in life, a person responds subjectively to a challenge. Taking care of the property is a necessity, a privilege, a release, a form of exercise, and a joy. I only feel that way about my own property. Pushing a mower or pulling a rake for half a day, at home, is therapy and superb exercise.

EPILOGUE

In becoming acquainted with the staff at Lincoln Center in New York City, I had luncheon with the director of personnel. We discovered that we had both played baseball. He was a first baseman in the New York Giants system and became well established in the minors. It was a pleasure, which incorporated nostalgia, to compare notes.

The contemporary idiocy of the world of professional sports is manifest; however, the personal exposure to a sport, or to a person who participated in a sport, creates a unique bonding. Relating to a stranger who represents a common interest in a specific sport is superior to cocktails for two. It facilitates conversation, and invokes memories, but does not necessarily create a friendship.

The bonding of athletics also applies to family relationships. Teaching a son to throw a baseball or football, or introducing a daughter to a track event, creates a special frisson. In the spring, when the first baseball was thrown in practice, the euphoria was palpable.

In the United States, organized sports, as we know them, have a limited history. Most contemporary sports were devised in the nineteenth century, and the changes have been profound. Generally, those changes are reasonable with two notorious exceptions. Commercialism, and the inordinate payments for services rendered, are destroying the joy of sports. Unless greed can be reduced, contemporary sports will not survive until the twenty-second century.

Other Books by Glenn W. Ferguson

Unconventional Wisdom, A Primer of Provocative Aphorisms,
     PenArtPro, 1999.

Americana Against the Grain, a Collection of Essays, PenArtPro, 1999.

Tilting at Religion, Prometheus Books, New York, 2003.

Travel with a Twist , Sunstone Press, 2005.

Printed in the United States
20640LVS00001B/79-129